Quantum Warrior

THE FUTURE OF THE MIND

Quantum Warrior

THE FUTURE OF THE MIND

JOHN KEHOE

ZOETIC INC., VANCOUVER

Zoetic Inc.
PO Box 48823
Bentall Centre
595 Burrard Street
Vancouver, British Columbia
Canada V7X 1A6
www.learnmindpower.com

Library and Archives Canada Cataloguing in Publication
Kehoe, John
    Quantum warrior : the future of the mind / John Kehoe.

Includes bibliographical references.
Issued also in electronic format.
ISBN 978-0-9739830-3-6
1. Self-actualization (Psychology). 2. Mind and body. I. Title.

BF637.S4K439 2011   158.1   C2011-904555-9

Printed in Canada

Contents

Acknowledgements

I always struggle with an acknowledgement page, not because of who to include but who not to include. It sounds like a cliché, but as a writer and a man dedicated to self-knowledge, every person and event in my life has meaning and significance. Every person I meet adds to who I am, influences how I see the world, and in a very real way finds themselves in these pages.

Do I include Alice and Ray, my masseuse and masseur, who experienced my excitement and despair (depending on how it was going) week by week during the writing process? Do I include those teachers, intellectuals, mystics and visionaries who have inspired me through their books, teachings, lectures, and sometimes personal friendships? Speaking of friendships, what about the many friends and associates who have listened to my musings on the contents of this book and whose responses and ideas have been invaluable? And my students and loyal readers in many countries who have corresponded with me through my website and attended my seminars; surely they must be acknowledged as providing source material and inspiration. Not to mention spiritual sources, ancestors, parents, siblings; the list goes on and on. As you can see, there are many sources of inspiration that have been "grist for the mill" of this book and many people who deserve my appreciation. All of the above are gratefully acknowledged.

I must also thank Jennifer and Ric Beairsto for their editing, copy proofing, and encouragement. Editors play a critical role in bringing the best out of a writer and this book reflects their efforts. I further thank Christine Hwang for the cover design and Kate Moore for the layout. Finally I want to thank my wife, who reads my first drafts and is always ruthlessly honest in her appraisal. Besides acting as what I call "the first editor," she supplied me with inspiration and ideas at all stages of the book. She is my best friend, lover, spouse and almost constant companion, and I am a blessed man for having her in my life. Thank you all.

John Kehoe

ONE

Mind Power

"Life is an instrument and
we must learn how to play it."
{ Credo Mutwa }

We live in extraordinary times, where science is revealing truths about the universe that are both startling and breathtaking. Our universe, it now appears, is a place where black holes swallow galaxies, subatomic particles interconnect with each other intuitively, past and future interchange with one another, and where space curves and warps around the physical objects contained within it.[1] The most up-to-date findings of physics suggest that everything consists of vibrating strings of energy, and the dimension we perceive as space and time may well exist within a multidimensional universe, perched on a giant membrane, side by side with other dimensions we have yet to discover.[2]

If this was a science fiction novel you would not be faulted for dismissing it all as pure fantasy, but this is not a novel, nor is it fiction, but rather the staggering new reality being revealed to us by the brightest minds in science. Yet, as incredible and fantastic as all this is, perhaps the greatest mystery being resolved may well turn out to be the enigma of our place in the whole scheme of this evolving universe. The age-old question has always been the same: Are human beings just insignificant accidents of nature, birthed from the quantum soup with no particular purpose or meaning, or are we something much grander, with cosmic destinies yet to be discovered? There are many scientists, and lay individuals as well, arguing convincingly and passionately on both sides of this question, but as we will discover, there is new, compelling evidence to suspect that there is much more to who we are than any of us could have previously dared to imagine. While philosophers and mystics for thousands of years have struggled to understand the purpose and meaning of our lives, paradoxically, it is now science that is helping us to understand who we are, and where our place in the universe can be found.

What we know is that we are complex and extraordinary beings of consciousness and energy. There is a dynamic and symbiotic relationship that exists between consciousness and energy, but it is only quite recently that scientists have discovered how this relationship works.[3] While physicists for some time have known that all physical reality is made up of vibrating energy, few had suspected that consciousness was also part of the system. Scientists always thought that consciousness had nothing to do with matter or energy other than as a subjective means to interpret what was happening around us, but this perspective has changed dramatically, and now consciousness is seen as an intricate part in the entire scheme of things. Consciousness, we now know, plays a much bigger role in creating our reality than anyone had previously expected.

The fields of neurobiology, quantum physics, string theory, depth psychology and neuroplasticity, to name but a few, are exploding with new discoveries relevant to understanding who we are. These new discoveries are not only intellectually stimulating; they nurture our very souls with the breathtaking vision they present. Understanding these findings can help us live our lives with greater vision and effectiveness, yet the plethora of information is so overwhelming that it is difficult to know where to begin.

Through neuroplasticity, for example, we now know the brain can be rewired using conscious intention. Depth psychology teaches us that we have two minds, and that our second, subconscious mind contains shadow patterns which capture energy from us until they are discovered and integrated.[4] Quantum physics tells us that we are living in a vast sea of energy, where everything is connected.[5] It further reveals that past, present and future are happening simultaneously.[6] But what is even more exciting, and perhaps the greatest of all the new discoveries, from a practical point of view, is that we now have indisputable proof that our consciousness has the ability to direct energy.[7] Since everything in the known universe consists of energy, the implications of this finding are staggering.

We are fortunate to be living in the twenty-first century where these cutting-edge discoveries are being revealed, for it gives us the opportunity to use them in ways our predecessors could never have imagined. If we had a methodology to put all this information together in a practical way, the possibilities of what could be done with it are astounding. Literally everything becomes possible when we embrace these theories and live *in a quantum way*.

It is fascinating to look back at my life and realize that I have spent over forty years devoting myself to understanding consciousness and using it in unique and creative ways. In 1978 I developed one of the first mind power training systems and began travelling the world sharing these methods. In 1987 I wrote a best-selling book about my work called *Mind Power*.[8] The method I taught combined the powers of thought with the laws of *quantum reality*.

Quantum reality is the reality that exists beyond our senses.[9] It is the invisible framework of energy that creates our universe. It holds the molecules in a chair stable so that we may sit on it; it directs and determines where a cyclone will hit, and when an earthquake will happen. It is the invisible framework of everything we experience. What is not commonly understood, however, is that our thoughts and quantum reality are very intimately related with one another. Consciousness, as incredible as it sounds, directs energy. To know this is to know something great.

The laws of the universe are set up perfectly for us to avail ourselves of them. We have been designed and hardwired to make use of these laws. Our brain, the motherboard of our consciousness, is neurologically programmed to assist us in working with these laws, providing us with the opportunities to use them in innumerable creative ways. We are designed for success. Success is an inherent part of the universe, for without the laws of energy and consciousness working together successfully, the universe would fall apart. And the laws that operate in the universe operate in our lives as well, for we are a microcosm of the macrocosm, a universe in miniature.[10] The same laws that govern the galaxies govern individual people and nations, as we are all part of this evolving universe and cannot be separated from it.

However, the laws of the universe are not always easily understood, especially when they are first introduced to us. Some quantum truths about our reality seem so incredible that they shake our present view of ourselves and the world we live in, but they are supported by the most up-to-date scientific facts and must be incorporated into our understanding of who we are if we wish to be in harmony with the universe.

The most fundamental scientific fact of our reality is, however, a very easy concept to understand. Everything that we experience in our life is made up of vibrating energy. All physical reality that we see and feel, such as chairs, houses, people, trees, oceans, even our own bodies, while appearing solid to our senses, are made up of vibrations of energy. Everything in the universe consists of vibrating energy. Everything! Our feelings, thoughts, beliefs and desires also consist of this vibrating energy. This is what we call the first understanding of our reality.

The second understanding is that consciousness directs this energy. Consciousness and energy are in relationship with one another. So from these two simple scientific truths we have the starting point to begin to work creatively with mind power. Later, as we begin training and practicing the quantum techniques, we will contemplate these truths many times, imprinting them into our subconscious where they will become resonating patterns of energy, active and dynamic parts of who we are. These two understandings will become a permanent part of our evolving quantum model;[11] they will assist us in creating success for ourselves. Again, each of us has been designed, wired and programmed to be successful, and we must always remember this. The laws of the universe are designed to facilitate success, and we are encouraged to create and apply these laws, each in our own unique way. It is through our successes that the universe creatively expresses itself.

Working with the quantum laws, we discover our oneness with energy. Doing this opens up a whole different way of working with energy, and we discover that we can easily direct energy with our thoughts. Most of us have no idea of how to do this. It is not taught in school, nor is it common knowledge. In fact, if we are honest with ourselves, most of us will admit that our thoughts are the last thing we actually think about. We go through our waking hours taking little notice of our thought processes: how the mind moves, what it fears, what it heeds, what it says to itself, what it brushes aside. For the most part we eat, converse, worry, hope, plan, make love, shop, work and play, all with minimal attention paid to how we think. This is unfortunate, for we are neglecting one of the most important and powerful forces in our life.

Mind power teaches us how to direct our thoughts with will and imagination towards a particular purpose. By holding in our mind images of what we want to happen in our life, we are vibrating a specific energy. In consciousness we can vibrate any energy we choose, and in doing so we *weave the web*. 'Weaving the web' is an expression I will use throughout this book, and it means we interact with the quantum web of energy, what I will call *the energy web*. Physicists call the energy web the quantum vacuum,[12] a misnomer if there ever was one. The quantum vacuum is not a vacuum at all—every part of it contains vast amounts of energy and information. The term 'energy web' gives the mind a more accurate way of imagining the web's properties, and also acts as a symbol for what is possible. Symbols, we will learn, carry their own power, so it is to our advantage to refer to the quantum vacuum in this way.

The energy web is filled with energy and information, and contains within it unlimited possibilities of manifestation. Each of us can weave the web any time we choose, and we can do this consciously, fully aware of what we are doing. For example, when we focus our thoughts on successful outcomes in our life we are weaving the web, increasing the probability of these events happening. Everything in the universe has its own unique vibration, what scientists call its energy signature,[13] and when we consistently activate this vibration through daily practices, this energy will weave the web in a way that will attract these circumstances to us. Put in the most basic terms, what we focus on we attract.

Now, of course, there is more to it than this simple explanation, and I don't want to give the impression that everything we wish and hope for we can achieve simply by thinking about it, but this is the starting point in understanding the unique relationship that exists between the energy web and our own consciousness. Our thoughts are the most powerful creative forces in our life. Learning to work with thoughts in quantum ways—beyond simple positive thinking—awakens for us a whole new life of power and opportunity.

Let me share with you the very first time I experimented with weaving the web using this system. In sharing this story, you will understand what is possible when we apply the laws of consciousness and energy in a systematic way. I am going back almost forty years. I was in my late twenties and had built a cabin in the woods of British Columbia where I was living, sorting through the extensive research I had gathered on the powers of the mind during the previous three years. The cabin overlooked a marsh where beavers had built a dam, and I would hear them working at night, slapping the water with their tails as they packed mud and branches together in a never-ending process of dam building and rebuilding. It was a very serene, peaceful environment, perfect for my purposes. I was trying to design a system of mind power that I could easily apply in my life. Up till this point, all the information I had was conceptual and theoretical. I had not yet demonstrated mind power to any noticeable degree. This was about to change radically.

Even though I was living frugally, my money had run out, so to make ends meet I was doing odd jobs in order to earn enough for basic groceries and kerosene for my lamps. I was struggling financially, and then one night I suddenly decided that this was ridiculous. If these theories of consciousness and energy that I was reading about were true, I thought to myself, I should be able to create anything in my life, including an abundance of money. At least I shouldn't be broke. Why am I struggling? I wondered. So I decided to take action and put these theories to a test. I must admit there was a feeling of both excitement and trepidation with this decision. What if it didn't work? This would disprove everything I believed in. If it doesn't work, then better to move on and not waste any more of my time I thought, dismissing my doubts, and so with this resolve I began to put my system of mind power into practice.

I must explain something more about energy before I continue my story, as it will help explain why this system is so powerful. As mentioned previously, everything has its own unique vibration of energy, its vibrational signature. The energy of confidence, for example, has a very specific vibrational resonance, just as the colour red has a different spectral vibration from the colour green or blue. Whenever we vibrate with confidence we align ourselves with this particular energy. We literally become that energy. A mother who is confidently playing with her children is aligning with the exact same energy as a businessman who is confidently closing a hundred million dollar deal, or a professional athlete who is about to execute an amazing play with assurance. While the circumstance in which the confidence is being employed is different in each case, the vibration of the energy is exactly the same.

Understanding this principle, I decided to align myself with the energy of abundance. To do this I trained my mind to think abundance by recognizing and acknowledging abundance wherever I saw it. Rather than try to create an abundance of money, which I had very little of, I made the practice more all-inclusive, figuring that aligning with abundance energy would activate all abundance, including financial abundance. It was sort of a back-door approach. So whenever I saw or experienced any type of abundance, even an abundance of wild flowers at the side of the road, I would acknowledge this abundance, and vibrate for several moments with this energy, absorbing and aligning with that energy.

I knew theoretically that aligning myself with this energy should attract abundance to me. At least that was my reasoning. It's funny to be looking back to those times, so many years ago, because at that point in my life I had no firsthand experience in working with energy. Now, of course, it is second nature to me, but back then I was young, naïve and filled with confidence, which was a good thing too, because working with energy in these ways is quite radical even today, when so much more is known about this science. Back then no one really understood why or even if it worked.[14]

I had also discovered that the subconscious mind could not tell the difference between what is real and what is imagined, that it would accept whatever impressions and vibrations I resonated with and work with that particular energy.[15] This practice should translate the energy of abundance into the physical equivalent for me; at least this is what I was hoping. So I practiced aligning with abundance daily, wherever and whenever I had the opportunity. It was actually very simple how I brought this practice into my life, and I have shared this story in my book *Mind Power into the 21st Century*, but not in this detail or with these explanations. For example, when I was eating grapes—because that was all I could afford—I would say to myself, "Look, I don't have just one grape. I don't have just two grapes. I have an abundance of grapes to eat." When I said this to myself it felt truthful; it was abundance and I was aligning myself to it, even if it was only grapes that were abundant in my life. Now you could argue that I could just as easily have been thinking to myself, "I'm so broke that all I can afford to eat tonight is fruit." And you would be absolutely right, that too was my reality, but through choice I aligned myself with the energy of abundance. Choice, you will discover, is a powerful tool, and with quantum mind power we use it in ways most people could not imagine. The ability to choose what we think and so direct our thoughts is a creative act of volition of enormous significance.

I cooked my meals and heated the cabin with a woodstove. At the side of the cabin was a cord of wood that I had previously cut and stacked. Every time I went to get wood for the stove, which was several times a day, I would say to myself, "Look, I don't have just one piece of wood. I don't have just two pieces of wood. I have an abundance of wood." When I went out for a walk I would say to myself, "Look at the abundance of beauty around me. The trees, the sounds, the water, the animals; there is an abundance of beauty all around me." Whenever I looked up at the night sky I reminded myself of the abundance of stars and galaxies, the immenseness of it all. When I travelled to town, which I did once a week to buy my meagre basics, I would look at the large buildings and remind myself that there were corporations that owned these buildings that were extraordinarily successful and abundant. In my imagination I aligned myself with this energy and vibrated this abundance. I didn't want to own the buildings myself, but I could vibrate abundance by thinking of the people who might own them, becoming their vibration of abundance in my imagination. To resonate with these vibrations in our mind is not simply daydreaming, but a method of working with energy which weaves the web. Our will and imagination can work together in remarkable ways when we activate them towards a specific purpose.

This practice of aligning with abundance, though strange at first, eventually became quite effortless for me. I enjoyed doing it and I did it often, many times a day. It took only moments at a time, whenever opportunities presented themselves to me. I did this with all parts of my life. I reminded myself that I had an abundance of friends, an abundance of health, an abundance of knowledge. It became for me a regular practice of aligning with abundance. Actually, abundance became my favourite word and I used it a lot. I liked the sound and feel of the word and it vibrated within me every time I used it. The reality of my situation, if you were to look at it logically, was that I was dead-broke, no money, no opportunities, with no ideas on how to change this, but still I vibrated abundance every day, many times a day. I thought abundance, spoke abundance, connected with abundance . . . and then the most remarkable thing happened. It began happening to me.

It came first as an idea. One evening I suddenly realized that I could teach this mind power system to others. The idea was so clear; resonating with such intensity that I knew this was what I should do. My first couple of talks were at public libraries, where I worked out my ideas and honed my speaking skills,[16] and then in April 1978 I booked a conference room in the most prestigious hotel in Victoria, the Empress, even though I could not afford it (I borrowed the money). I advertised in the local media and presented my concepts to an eager audience who packed the room to capacity. My four-part lecture series, called "Thought Dynamics," was incredibly popular right from the beginning, and the public response was extraordinary. Within the first year I was attracting large crowds to my talks, often in excess of a thousand people. People were fascinated with this new methodology, and I began the first of what would be many world tours. Money was flowing in.

Fast-forward five years from the day I left the cabin. I am touring Australia for the second time and have checked into the presidential suite at the Sheraton Hotel in Sydney. It is the same suite the Beatles had stayed in when they played Sydney. I remember the thrill of walking around the suite, imagining them being there. The suite had a large living room with floor-to-ceiling windows overlooking the Sydney Opera House. It was gorgeous, extravagant, lavish, abundant, certainly more than was needed for just one person, and then the thought hit me. In five short years I had come from a cabin in the woods, with no electricity and no running water, to the presidential suite of the Sheraton Hotel, and I had checked in for an entire month. A month! In that moment it suddenly dawned on me how extraordinary the system was, and how the abundance vibration which I had decided to align with five years previously was now a part of who I was. It had happened in ways I could have never imagined.[17]

The reason I'm telling you this particular story is that I want to get your attention. I want you to know that mind power is not just some intellectual concept to me. It is a system of techniques I have used effectively in my life with astounding success, and taught to millions of others through my books and lectures. Mind power works because it harnesses the known laws of the universe in easily applicable ways that anyone can learn to use.

To know and understand the universe we must know and understand ourselves. This is why knowledge about the universe, while intellectually interesting, will not help us in any meaningful way until we understand ourselves. There is only one way of doing this, and that is by coming into a relationship with all parts of ourselves. In the quantum mind power system, which is an advanced system based on my original mind power training, we learn to feel with our bodies, intuit with our souls, weave energy with our minds, and harness the hidden powers of our subconscious. We access all parts of ourselves and in doing so we discover the meaning of our lives.

In 2002 I stopped all teaching and began a three-year listening sabbatical.[18] I was mentored during this period by an extraordinary woman, a mystic, who had listened deeply, pierced through the mysteries of life and had secrets to share with me. You will meet her later in the book. Through listening I discovered new and different ways of working with energy. Through my mentor's guidance I learned to feel energy and to come into relationship with it. This was a very different and powerful way of working with energy that I had not used before. It was also during this period that I deepened my relationship with the different parts of myself, awakening my body, subconscious and soul. It was a remarkable time, and if I were to sum up the experience in one word, the word would be relationship. Through listening I discovered what many before me have discovered—we are in relationship with everything—and as I deepened my relationships, remarkable things began happening. It was during this three-year sabbatical that a whole new set of techniques evolved, and the vision of being a quantum warrior revealed itself to me. A unique methodology of working with energy and consciousness emerged, and through these new techniques I learned what is possible when we train and live in an extraordinary way.

TWO

Consciousness

"This brain ... small space
but lots of mystery there."
{ Dalai Lama }

In 1995, neuroscientist Alvaro Pascual-Leone conducted a series of experiments at the Harvard Medical School that have gone largely unnoticed by the general public, yet the implications of what he found are staggering, changing forever how we should view ourselves. In controlled settings, Pascual-Leone had a group of volunteers practice a simple five-finger piano exercise as fluidly as they could. Each day for five days, the volunteers practiced on the piano for two hours, and after each day's practice they underwent a transcranial magnetic stimulation (TMS), which allowed the scientists to observe their brain functions. The TMS mapped the motor cortex of each participant, and after a week of practice, the scientists observed new circuits being created. The physical act of playing the piano was rewiring the brain. This in itself, while intriguing, was not that surprising; in fact it was expected. There had been a growing body of evidence suggesting that repeated physical actions have an affect on the neural circuitry of the brain, and this experiment further verified these findings.[1]

It was in the next experiment where things became fascinating. Pascual-Leone had a comparable group do a similar exercise, only this time instead of playing the piano they were instructed to merely think about playing it. They played the exact same piece of music in their heads, holding their hands still but imagining each finger movement as if they were actually making it. Amazingly, the mental rehearsal showed the same degree of new circuitry being created as was brought about by physical practice. Motor circuits became active simply through the process of mental imagery. Like actual physical movements, imagined movements trigger synaptic change at the cortical level. Merely thinking about moving the fingers produced brain changes comparable to those triggered by actually moving those fingers.[2]

This startling discovery showed that the neural activity of the brain and the contents of our consciousness are linked. The importance of this discovery cannot be overstated. The key finding of Pascual-Leone is that the brain wires itself in response to signals it receives from its environment, and that these signals can be *self-directed* by consciousness. I have italicized the previous words because this ability to rewire our neural circuitry is of enormous significance. In discovering this truth about ourselves we have unlocked a code that has been hidden from mankind for the entire existence of our species. Now that this code has been revealed, the genie is out of the bottle, and the possibilities of what we might do with this extraordinary mind-brain relationship are breathtaking.

And if this isn't enough, the mystery of the brain deepens even further. Many brain researchers now suspect that the brain itself is a form of hologram.[3] A hologram is an entity where the whole is contained in each and all of the pieces. In holographic photography, for example, you can take a photograph of a flower and break that photographic plate in half and you will see not half the flower but two pictures of the whole flower. Break it in four and you have four pieces, each depicting the whole flower. This continues into smaller and smaller pieces, into infinity. As you reduce the size, the picture becomes less and less discernible, but it still contains the whole picture.

When we speak of the brain as holographic we mean that any part of the brain, even a single cell, reflects or encompasses the workings of the total brain. This likelihood is actively being explored by neuroscientists, but an even more intriguing possibility, however fantastic it seems, is that each human brain may in fact be a holographic piece of the entire universe.

This would sound too incredible to even consider were it not that similar theories are elaborated upon in many of the world's great religions. The Jewish Kabbalah, for example, teaches that each human being is a microcosm of the macrocosm, or "a little universe in miniature." Kabbalah[4] is the mystical branch of Judaism consisting of an elaborate body of work whereby both man and the universe are divided into ten different spheres, or energy sources, that interact with one another to create our reality. The whole process is called "the Tree of Life." Through accessing these sources and the powers they contain, we hold the keys to understanding ourselves and the cosmos. According to this ancient mystical teaching, all forces contained in the vast outer universe are contained within each human being. We are fragmented holographic pieces of the entire cosmos, and as such we have access to everything that has ever been or ever will be.

My interest in spirituality and metaphysics began almost forty years ago when I more or less stumbled upon these teachings while researching consciousness. I was surprised at the wealth of information that the great religions and shamanic teachings possessed about consciousness. True, you often needed to separate the dogma from the core essence of what was taught, but nonetheless, the depth of understanding of how consciousness interacts with our physical world was remarkable, and all the more impressive given that many of these teachings date back thousands of years. Most of the great spiritual traditions, I discovered, contain sophisticated methodologies for accessing hidden wisdom and working with the powers of the universe, even if these teachings are often cryptically hidden in metaphor and parable.[5] The religious traditions I will draw upon most often in this book are Christianity, Buddhism and Kabbalah. I have chosen these three because they are the ones I am most familiar with and, conveniently, they fit perfectly with the quantum holographic model. Some readers may choose to dismiss spiritual sources, claiming they are unreliable and unscientific, but these teachings do add another perspective, a deeper layer of understanding in helping us decipher the mystery of who we are and where our place in the universe lies. In my search for understanding, I was certainly not prepared to dismiss any relevant information, regardless of source, especially since these teachings were so captivating from a quantum perspective.

But it's not just religions that put forth the holographic model of consciousness; many scientists have now moved in this direction as well. Neurologist Richard Restak, author of the bestseller *The Brain*, which was the basis for a PBS series, holds strongly the opinion that "a hologram is not only possible, but at this moment represents probably our best model for brain functioning." Restak, like countless other scientists and researchers in this field, is in awe of the brain's abilities, and why wouldn't he be? The 'motherboard' of our consciousness, the human brain is an extraordinary masterpiece of creation. Nothing in the known universe is more complicated or intricate, and the possibilities of what it is capable of are still being discovered. We are nowhere near to understanding its potential. What we do know is that the brain has been hardwired for maximum potential and effectiveness.

To understand the mechanics of our brain we begin by examining the role neurons play in its development. Neurons carry information, and without neurons our brain could not function, so nature ensures that there is no shortage by producing neurons at a prodigious rate soon after our conception. Incredibly, by the seventh week of gestation, our newly formed brain, growing by leaps and bounds in the embryo, is producing five hundred thousand neurons a minute. Functional circuits begin appearing almost everywhere within the brain.

At birth our brain contains some one hundred billion nerve cells, and each of these one hundred billion cells connects to thousands of more neurons, sometimes even one hundred thousand more. By the time we leave the womb, a conservative number of the wired connections is one hundred trillion. Scientist Gerald Edelman claims the human cortex alone has thirty billion neurons capable of making a million billion synaptic connections.[6] It is no wonder that the human brain is often described as the most complex known object in the universe, and there is every reason to believe that many of its functions are still to be discovered.

This wiring together of millions of neurons into functional circuits is reflected in the maxim, "Neurons that fire together wire together." This is known as Hebb's Law, and it is one of the keys to understanding both neuroplasticity and the powers of the mind.[7] We will come to greatly appreciate the brain's ability to wire itself in innovative ways as we incorporate these processes within the quantum mind power techniques.

Until recently, the brain's ability to rewire itself in uniquely creative and innovative ways was largely ignored by the scientific community, mostly because there was little understanding of how or why it worked. This has changed dramatically in the twenty-first century, and the new frontier of neuroplasticity has neuroscientists and neurobiologists excited about the potentials it holds, and rightly so. What we are discovering is that the practices of neuroplasticity, combined with the laws of quantum reality, open up new and undreamed of possibilities that until quite recently could never have even been conceived of, much less implemented.

Neuroplasticity is an impressive-sounding word, but really it describes a very simple process. It refers to the ability of neurons to always forge new connections. Neuroplasticity, at its essence, is the process of the brain wiring and rewiring itself.

Actually it was Sigmund Freud who first suspected that the brain had neuroplastic capabilities, and he wrote extensively on the possibilities. In 1895, more than fifty years before Donald Hebb postulated his famous law, Freud was working with the concept of synapses connecting with one another, writing articles explaining how we are changed by what we learn, experience and program into ourselves. It is not well known, but Freud actually began his career as a laboratory neuroscientist, and only shifted to taking clients in private practice in order to support himself and his family. It is ironic, but had laboratory work paid better and he had remained in his original career, he might never have developed the incredible body of work he was to create on the subconscious.[8] However, Freud's concepts of neural wiring profoundly shaped his thinking, and were a foundation for all his later psychoanalytic methods.

This astounding process of neural wiring is in full momentum throughout all stages of the forming embryo. However, the moment we leave the womb a whole new set of dynamics begins. The shaping and wiring of our brain is now influenced by our environment, setting in motion a process that ultimately determines who we will become as individuals. Not only are there more synapses and neurons being created, but they are now being ruthlessly pruned away as well. By one estimate, twenty billion synapses are pruned every day between childhood and early adolescence.[9] Which synapses remain and which are pruned depends entirely on whether the circuits carry any traffic. It is survival of the busiest. Connections that are used become stronger, becoming permanent elements of the brain's circuitry, and those that are not used are pruned away.

The growth of our consciousness is facilitated by a series of formation shifts both biological and interactive. We are designed to grow in intelligence by exploring and interacting with our environment. Each interaction creates a shift of understanding, propelling us into another set of unknown, unpredictable experiences, which are in turn processed and assimilated. Through this never-ending progression our intelligence grows.

In his book *The Developing Mind*, Dr. Daniel Siegel wrote, "For the growing brain of a young child, the social world supplies the most important experiences influencing the expression of genes, which determines how neurons connect to one another in creating the neurological pathways which give rise to mental activity."[10] Our environment provides us with not just our experiences, but also effectively wires the brain as we process this information. Each new experience registers within the brain, firing and wiring neurons as our evolving consciousness interprets and summarizes each event. This inner tapestry of neurons firing and synapses connecting, forming into circuits, is being orchestrated by the signals the brain receives from our experiences. Each new experience is assimilated and incorporated into the system.[11]

The formation of our mind's consciousness is an extraordinary process. It is through the myriad of daily experiences that personal consciousness evolves. Our brain has the ability to rapidly download an unimaginable amount of content, and in the process it forms our behaviours and beliefs.

We are designed to grow and be strengthened by every event, no matter how mundane or awesome. The never-ending flow of experiences—people, successes, failures, catastrophes and triumphs—all play their part in this development. An incredible capacity for innovation and change is built within us, and this capacity propels us into new and different circumstances as we constantly seek out opportunities to express our creative power. This complex process of information gathering creates what we refer to as our *inventory*. As a new human we are born with a driving intent to express ourselves and gain inventory. This gathering of inventory goes on our entire life. It never stops.

The diversity of our environment and our interpretation of our experiences are what make us who we are. While we all possess a collective unconscious[12] and with it a collective wisdom which has been inherited from our lineage, our own personal consciousness, the one that thinks, makes decisions and is self-reflective, is a unique creation of its own making, and this is how the universe wants it. We are meant to be unique.

Our interactions, both physical and psychological, bring about a patterning in our brain whereby our concepts are formed and encoded within. The values and beliefs we observe in our parents and primary caregivers become an early and powerful stimulus, and often are assimilated and hardwired within. We become not only what our environment presents to us, but even more so how we interpret our experiences. The power of suggestion is overwhelming in this critical early stage of development. What is presented to us will be accepted, especially if the stimulus is repeated many times. The imprints recorded by a child being told he is stupid, funny looking or bad are assimilated within and take on a subconscious pattern. Because our psyche intuitively knows we are extraordinary, it comes as a double shock to us to learn that we are bad, stupid, can't draw, funny looking, awkward, or a host of other imprints we may mistakenly gather into our inventory. Many of our limitations today have their roots in false programming from a very early age.

These harmful messages become hardwired in our brains, and here is where the problem arises: much of what we accept as true and accurate will in fact be faulty and limiting, and yet it will become part of our inner programming. Our newly formed consciousness, hungry for content, is downloading everything presented to it, and misconceptions and faulty programs are inevitable side effects of this process, becoming active parts of what I call our *model of reality*.

The term model of reality refers to the way our mind constructs reality using concepts it can understand. Our model of reality is what creates meaning for us, and each of us creates our own particular model of reality. While there will be overlapping similarities between all our models, each of us has a unique way in which we interpret our different life experiences. Some models are quite dysfunctional, causing problems as these programs act out their patterns. For example, if a person believes that nothing good happens to them, or that life is filled with hardships and disappointment, not only will this be the lens through which they view the panorama of their experiences, but these beliefs will also create a vibrating energy pattern attracting these very circumstances to them. On the other hand, some individuals have models of reality that are extraordinarily empowering, quite visionary, and these too influence what happens to those who hold these models. While all of our models of reality are initially created unconsciously, in that we are totally unaware of the process as it is happening to us, there comes a point in our life when we awaken to who we are, and we set in motion a process that actively rewires our circuits in new, more cosmic, visionary ways.

While we are gathering inventory and creating a model of reality, a weave of circuitry is developing within our brain as it assimilates all the information it is receiving. But there is another hidden system at work here as well, one that most scientists have ignored but which psychologists know all too well. The heartache, success, victory and betrayal, the sickness and disappointment, all weave themselves within our subconscious mind via an invisible cosmic loom. Our subconscious synthesizes, abstracts and forms its own conclusions, creating its own inventory and model of reality. As it turns out, we have two minds, with two different models of reality, one conscious and one subconscious. This is an astounding development, and one that we are largely unaware of. The inventory of our subconscious will be of great interest to us as we embark on the path of self-knowledge, for it influences every aspect of our life. We will explore this in greater detail in a later chapter.

Some children will become confident, others timid and fearful, according not only to their experiences but to their interpretations of these experiences on both a conscious and subconscious level. A child raised in an abusive atmosphere might conclude that life is unsafe, that he or she is unworthy, and wire this within. Another child may experience a failure or dramatic incident which causes an imprint to develop within that engenders a sense of hopelessness and despair. Strangely enough, the exact same set of circumstances can cause an imprint of determination, a burning desire to succeed in a different child. Why it goes one way or another is still a mystery, but each consciousness processes experiences in its own unique manner.[13]

Until quite recently it was thought that the hardwiring of neural activity ended in early childhood.[14] This belief continued well into the late 1990s, when scientists at several institutions[15] shocked the world of neuroscience with the discovery that there is a second major phase of activity just before puberty, and yet another in the early twenties when the circuitry rewires itself yet again.[16] Now, we realize that the brain is a constant work in progress. The theory which stated that the adult brain is fixed and doesn't change is now so outdated that Dr. Norman Doidge, author of *The Brain That Changes Itself*, took to describing it this way: "Not only is this theory wrong but it is spectacularly wrong."[17]

Research now shows that the adult brain retains impressive powers of neuroplasticity, and that neural wiring continues throughout all stages of our life. This is excellent news. It means we can rewire ourselves at any point in our life.

Nature programs every new brain system, not just that of humans, for maximum potential. An extraordinary amount of information can be programmed into even the most basic brain systems. Most animal species, for example, have complex preprogrammed information about the world they will interact with, information which informs them on how to move and adapt successfully within that world. Once exposed to their environment, the innate programs within these species are quickly activated. Consider the salmon; its tiny brain has a built-in knowledge of the magnetic lines of force surrounding the earth, and it navigates by means of this knowledge. When the inner call to spawn occurs, salmon can find their way through thousands of miles of ocean, up hundreds of miles of fresh water to the very brook from which they came, and there they spawn. They access this built-in map of the world via their neural programming.

Likewise monarch butterflies, which migrate each fall thousands of kilometers from northeastern United States and Canada to special wintering sites in central Mexico. These monarchs, three to five generations removed from the original monarchs that migrated north from Mexico, navigate unerringly to a place they have never seen. Not just to the very same place from which their ancestors migrated, but often to the very same tree.

Other animal, bird and insect species have a diversity of equally remarkable abilities; each specifically designed to assist them in the environment they will encounter. We, the human species, like the rest of nature, are similarly spectacularly wired for our environment, but it now appears our environment consists of much more than what we originally suspected. It is not just the physical world that we see and touch; now we see that there may be a myriad of frequency domains beyond time and space. Nature, which programs each species for maximum efficiency, has built a vast and awesome program within us designed for purposes far beyond simply making a living, raising children and seeking personal happiness, as important and meaningful as these activities are to us. Within our genetic coding, we now suspect, are contained vast cosmic programs, as well as powers beyond our wildest imagination. It now appears that we may well be cosmic beings programmed with destinies and powers we have yet to imagine, and it is just now that we are discovering this.

THREE

Quantum Reality

"Anybody who is not shocked by
quantum theory does not understand it."
{ Niels Bohr }

In quantum reality everything we think we know and understand about the world we live in is turned upside down. In the quantum world we cease to exist in the ways we commonly think of ourselves existing, and instead morph into an energy system where everything is connected to everything else. This is a world of oneness, interconnectivity and pulsating energy fields. The laws of time and space are replaced by other laws that oftentimes seem illogical. The truth and wonder of our reality is more complex and mysterious than we could ever have imagined, and what is even more astounding about this quantum world is that energy is responsive in the most intimate ways to the power of our thoughts.

Up until quite recently science has used two separate theories to explain our reality, Einstein's theory of general relativity and quantum theory.[1] Neither theory by itself could fully explain all that occurs in our universe, so both were used even though they were also somewhat at odds with another. Then in the 1980s, string theory[2] burst upon the scene and helped bridge the gap between these two perspectives. String theory suggests that there are more dimensions than the one we appear to exist in, parallel universes, and that these are all held together by an elaborate and elegant composition of vibrating strings of energy. All well and good, but the problem was there were five different string theories, each with their own, often opposing concepts. There was dissent and confusion in the string-theory kingdom. This changed dramatically in 1995 when physicist Edward Witten, considered by many to be the greatest living physicist, stunned a conference of physicists at the University of Southern California with what he called his "M-theory."[3]

No one was quite sure what the *M* stood for. Some suggested magic, others mystery and matrix, and there are even a few who thought it might be Witten's sense of humor, that the *M* was an upside-down *W* for Witten. Witten himself refused to reveal this. What he did, however, was combine all the available material of the various string theories and conclude that we are probably living on a giant membrane in a multidimensional space where there are far more dimensions than anyone had previously suspected. Eleven to be exact, and more dimensions give us more degrees of freedom and possibility. This was indeed a stunning vision. At first it seems too outrageous to believe, but this is cutting-edge physics, backed by the most brilliant scientific minds on the planet.[4]

String theory and quantum theory both reveal reality as it actually is, each in their own way, but quantum theory was the first to challenge our assumptions, and quantum mechanics changed the way we see everything. Quantum theory created a paradigm shift in the way we view the physical world. The old classical model of physics that existed before quantum theory was built upon the three-hundred-year-old Newtonian model where bodies of matter, small and large, interacted with each other and everything was easily explained through cause and effect. It was a mechanical model where the universe unfolded with mathematical precision. But when quantum theory burst upon the scene seventy years ago, everything was turned upside down, and the models that were supposed to explain how our universe worked were suddenly exposed as fiction. The new model that emerged, however, was not as easily understandable as the old one, and the vision it presented to us seemed so strange that it appeared illogical at first.[5]

For example, subatomic particles, which were supposed to be like tiny bits of matter interacting with each other according to the known laws of physics, didn't behave that way at all. For one thing they had a dual nature to them, behaving sometimes as if they were particles and at other times as if they were waves. They also had a mysterious interconnection known as "nonlocality," in that they could show up almost anywhere.[6] Subatomic particles seemed chameleon-like, sometimes waves and sometimes particles, so modern physicists took to calling them "quanta," which includes both qualities. They are not in one place at one time: each single quanta is both "here" and "there," and can potentially show up anywhere in space-time. Even stranger was the astounding realization that until they are measured or observed, quanta have no definite characteristics, but instead exist simultaneously in several states at the same time. The only time quanta ever appear as particles are when we are observing them. When we observe quanta (through sophisticated experiments) they freeze into a form which we call a particle, but when we are not looking at them they shape-shift back into waves of energy.[7]

This is truly astounding. The most basic units of physical reality have no uniquely determinable location, and exist as waves of energy in a strange state of possibility spread throughout the grid system of our entire universe. Incredibly, it is our consciousness that seems to awaken quanta to life and turn them into "things." In some mysterious alchemical way that no one yet understands, our consciousness acts as a catalyst, transforming quanta waves into quanta particles. It is our consciousness interacting with the energy web that is creating the reality we experience.

This discovery rocked the scientific community. With this new information everything had to be reevaluated. Suddenly consciousness became much more interesting to scientists, and now had to be accounted for. Not only did it have to be accounted for; it appeared that consciousness was a major player in the whole scheme of things. This was quite a turn of events, for until quite recently scientists had insisted our minds were outside the laws of physics and really didn't count for anything. Now, we discover, the mind not only penetrates this quantum world, but also actively participates in it. This is revolutionary, but what excites me the most about what is happening in physics today is that it now appears that consciousness may finally be on the verge of being recognized as the enigmatic missing link in the search for the holy grail of all science—the Theory of Everything.

String theorists and quantum physicists have struggled for decades without success to find a theory that would fully explain the properties of all known phenomena. However, if you add the laws of consciousness to the known laws of energy and matter, you suddenly have something quite exquisite. I am not alone here in taking this perspective. There are many in the scientific community who now suspect that consciousness is the most subtle yet powerful of all the forces in the universe. We now know it interacts with reality in a myriad of ways, and its vast potentials are still being explored.

As much as we have discovered about the powers of consciousness, we are still in the frontier stages of understanding its full potential. If it turns out that consciousness is in fact the missing link, and many indicators now point in this direction, it would explain many of the mysteries that are still eluding scientists.

It was a paradigm shift for science to include consciousness as a major player in what happens to us, a shift that most of us have yet to make in our day-to-day lives, for we still act as if our outside reality is something separate and independent from ourselves. We need to catch up with science and change the way we view ourselves.

Everything we experience in our life as outside of ourselves happens because of interactions between the contents of our mind and the dynamics of the quantum energy field. Thinking, feeling, intuiting, willing, hoping, fearing, praying, visualizing; these are not just inner psychological processes confined within ourselves. They are real forces of energy pulsating through the entire web of universal energy, causing effects accordingly.

It is one thing to understand this conceptually, but how does it actually work? Physicist David Bohm, a protégé of Einstein's and one of the pioneers in quantum physics, came up with a unified theory of mind and matter which helps explain this situation. Bohm saw the world as one "unbroken wholeness." The universe was a vast web of energy exchange with a basic substructure containing all possible versions of all possible forms of matter. The universe was not some blind, mechanistic act of chance, but an open-ended, intelligent and purposeful system making use of an elaborate feedback process between organisms and itself. The unifying mechanism was the exchange of energy and information, which is transmitted everywhere at once.

In this model we are constantly exchanging both information and energy with the entire quantum field. This suggests something very profound about ourselves and the universe in which we live. Suddenly we realize that our capabilities of working within this system in creative and innovative ways are far more extensive than we had ever imagined. What this model is suggesting is that there is no separation between the universe and us; we are all intrinsically interconnected; we are all one. This is of course exactly what the mystics have been telling us for thousands of years, and now science is telling us this too.

Once consciousness reluctantly became accepted as a player in the quantum field, and let's be honest, many abhorred and fought these findings, scientists began wondering how strong was its influence and what were its limits? This is exactly what prompted physicist Robert G. Jahn, dean of the School of Engineering and Applied Science at Princeton University, to run his own rigorously regulated tests that would allow no room for ambiguity or chance.[8] To do this work he formed the Princeton Engineering Anomalies Research Lab, which became known as PEAR.

Brenda Dunne, a developmental psychologist from the University of Chicago, well respected for her work in consciousness, was hired to assist in these experiments. After considering all the possible options, they decided to use a random event generator, or REG. This machine would randomly select binary numbers of zeros or ones. Participants would then attempt to influence the results of the machine. During the experiment, each participant was asked to hold a mental intention imagining more ones in one segment, more zeros in the second segment, and to not attempt any influence in the third. The segments usually lasted thirty minutes, during which up to a million hits would occur. From the very beginning, as the results from the tests starting coming in, the researchers knew they were witnessing something astounding. For the first time under the most scientifically designed procedures, they were seeing proof of the power of the mind in action. In a twelve-year period PEAR collected the largest database ever assembled on mental intention. Using a process called meta-analysis, the PEAR team combined all the REG experiments and concluded that the odds of these results happening by chance were over a trillion to one.[9] In other words conscious intention was influencing what the machine was producing. In 2000, the prestigious U.S. National Research Council, reviewing all the REG data concluded that the REG trials could not be explained by chance. Something else was at work. The results were conclusive. Our thoughts and intentions have an effect in the physical world in a very real and tangible way, which is what quantum reality predicts.

Now that we understand that consciousness is part of the quantum field, and is constantly interacting with it, another fundamental question needs answering, namely, what exactly is consciousness and where did it come from? From a quantum point of view there are compelling reasons to suspect that consciousness is present throughout the entire universe, existing in every part of it no matter how small or seemingly insignificant, and that this consciousness, ours included, is connected to the whole and birthed from the same source, the mother cosmic-consciousness that has existed from the beginning of time. Esteemed Nobel laureate George Wald shares the same conclusion. "Mind," he said, "rather than emerging as a late outgrowth in the evolution of life, has existed always."[10]

Consciousness, as outrageous as it first sounds, might even have preceded the big bang. While some in the scientific community howl when this theory is brought forth, claiming there is no proof that this is so, all I can reply is that there is no proof that it is not either. Consciousness, it turns out, is more of a mystery than we originally suspected. What it is and where it came from are questions for both the scientist and the mystic, with neither having exclusivity in this domain.

As our understanding of consciousness expands, a new concept of our universe also emerges. Our present-day scientific models about the emergence of our universe adhere mostly to the big bang theory, which more or less states that our universe was created some 13.6 billion years ago when a giant explosion set in motion the cosmos. There is no overt reason to dispute this theory; however it somehow conveniently ignores a crucial point, namely, how could our universe be created out of nothing?

Physicist Alan Guth of MIT agrees.[11] "It's a problem," he acknowledges. "The classical form of Big Bang doesn't say anything about what happened before. What caused it to bang?"[12] It seems only logical to speculate that while the big bang undoubtedly created "our" universe, it is highly likely that something created the big bang, and this something is what is sometimes referred to as the metaverse (*meta* coming from classical Greek meaning "behind" or "beyond"). In other words, there is another universe behind or beyond the universe we inhabit, the Mother Universe which birthed our universe, and quite probably untold other universes as well. This idea is not new, and proponents of the string theory now suspect that this is exactly what happened. String theorists, which include some of the leading scientists of today, envision a universe where parallel universes exist side by side with our own, and that the big bang is just one of probably millions of other occurrences in this mysterious metaverse.

Quantum coherence points in this direction as well. Coherence is a well-known phenomenon and simply means that subatomic particles are able to cooperate with each other, but the kind of coherence now being discovered in the cosmos is more complex than we had originally thought. There appears an almost instant correlation among the parts or elements of this time-space system. This is what Einstein called "spooky action at a distance,"[13] and while aware of this phenomenon, it troubled him, for he had no answers for it. The coherence of our universe shows us that all the stars and galaxies are connected in some way. This indicates that a previous universe is likely to have informed the birth of our universe, much the same way the genetic code of our parents informed the conception and growth of who we are today. If this is the case, and more and more evidence is pointing this way, then the idea that consciousness preceded the big bang becomes not only possible but probable.

If consciousness indeed preceded the big bang, it is not such a stretch to imagine it might actually be the original cause. What this premise is seeking to accomplish, to borrow a quote from Einstein, is to find "the simplest possible scheme of thought that will bind together all observed facts."

It is not unreasonable to suspect that consciousness might have created the quantum vacuum (energy web). This would explain why consciousness is so connected to it. The quantum vacuum is commonly referred to as the foundation that generates all things in the known universe.

Physicist Bohm described the process of the quantum vacuum creating reality as "in-formation," suggesting a process where the energy that is "in" the energy web actually "forms" the recipient. The idea of an in-formed universe is a new way of looking at what is happening in our universe, and it presents a different way of viewing ourselves as well. With all reality being in-formed from the field, and everything connected with everything else, we can be "in touch" with any part of this system, whether it is something across the street or in another galaxy. We can access anything contained within this elaborate system and use it for whatever purpose we design. Consciousness that exists everywhere and is one with everything allows us to do this, when we know how.

This brings us to another important question. Who and what are we that we are able to do this? How should we now view ourselves? In one reality we are individualized human beings, raising families, working at jobs, living our lives in a time-space frequency domain. Yet simultaneously in quantum reality, we are energy systems vibrating in the vast quantum field which exists in a different frequency domain. We live in both these domains simultaneously, and both have to be accounted for in understanding our lives. We can view ourselves as physical human beings, or as a blur of interference patterns enfolded throughout the cosmic hologram; both are literally true and equally valid interpretations of what is happening to us.

Neuroscientist Karl Pribram explained this dual nature of our reality, in this way: "If you penetrate through and look at the universe with a holographic system, you arrive at a different view, a different reality. And that other reality can explain things that have hitherto remained inexplicable scientifically: paranormal phenomena, synchronicities, the apparently meaningful coincidence of events."[14] Pribram realized that taking the holographic model to its logical conclusions opened the door to the probability that objective reality—the world of cars, mountains, houses and cities—might not even exist, or at least not exist in the way we think it does. Was it possible, he wondered, that what the mystics had been saying for centuries was true; reality was *maya*, an illusion, and what was really out there was a vast resonating symphony of energy wave forms, a "frequency domain" that is transformed into the world as we know it only after our consciousness interacts with it?

In 1951, Bohm published his book *Quantum Theory*, and it became an instant classic. One of Bohm's most startling assertions was that the tangible reality of our everyday lives is really a kind of illusion. Underlying it is a deeper order of existence, a vast and more primary level of reality that gives birth to all the objects and appearances of our physical world. Bohm called this deeper level of reality "the implicate (meaning enfolded) order," and he referred to our own level of existence as the explicate or unfolded order. He used these terms because he saw all forms in the universe as the result of countless enfoldings and unfoldings between these two orders. Since everything in the cosmos arises from this process, he believed it is meaningless to view the universe as composed of "parts." Bohm preferred to describe the universe as a "holomovement,"[15] since the term hologram did not convey the dynamic and ever-active nature of what is actually happening. According to Bohm, intelligence is present not only in all of matter, but in energy, space, time, the fabric of the entire universe and everything we can conceive of. Bohm further speculated that there is no reason to believe this was the end of things. There may be other undreamed of orders beyond it, infinite stages of further development.

Michael Talbot, author of *The Holographic Universe*, put it this way, "Despite its apparent materiality and enormous size, the universe does not exist in and of itself, but is the stepchild of something far vaster and more ineffable. More than that, it is not even a major production of this vaster something, but is only a passing shadow, a mere hiccup in the greater scheme of things."[16]

Our universe a passing shadow, a mere hiccup in the greater scheme of things? Could this be possible? At first it seems outrageous, but from a quantum perspective not only could this be possible; it is more probable than not.

Another set of facts points in this direction as well. Every part of space is filled with different waves or strings of energy. When physicists calculated the minimum amount of energy that might be involved, they found, to their amazement, that empty space contains thousands of times more energy than the total energy of all the matter in the known universe.[17] Some physicists dispute these findings, refusing to take this calculation seriously. Obviously something must be in error. But maybe not. There is another possibility that could explain this discrepancy. Bohm believed that this finding pointed to the vast and hidden nature of the implicate order, to untold frequency domains beyond our perceptions. If our frequency domain of time and space is just one of thousands or maybe millions of other dimensions, this supposed error in energy calculation might in itself be the best proof yet that there are other worlds out there in different dimensions.

THE QUANTUM FIELD OF POSSIBILITIES

Since consciousness and energy work together, it should be possible for us to use this system as a blank canvas, imprinting into it whatever patterns we wish to create for ourselves. Might we use energy and consciousness the same way an artist uses a brush and paint, creating our own unique life experiences through our volition? Could this in fact be what the energy web was originally intended for from the beginning of time?

Kabbalistic teachings have something to say about the possibilities of combining energy and consciousness. In *Yesod*, which in the universe is the energy web, and in us the subconscious, this has very practical applications. I will explain the subconscious implications of how this works in a later chapter; however this is an opportunity to learn what this teaching says about the energy web. The initiation into this sphere, which is really a heightened awareness of how it works, brings with it an understanding of "the machinery of the universe." This description gives us a very interesting clue to how it works. From what we have discovered so far, we can see how understanding the energy web is indeed to see the machinery of the universe in action.

A further piece of Kabbalistic information also assists us in understanding the dynamics of energy. It is through the conscious mind that the "representations are designed and imprinted."[18] According to this ancient Jewish teaching, it is the mind that acts upon and imprints into the energy web whatever it wishes to manifest.

Following this line of thought, Jesus advises us to seek the kingdom of heaven and all else will be given to us.[19] It seems that when we find the kingdom of heaven we hold the keys to everything, but where do we look? Jesus further adds, "The kingdom of heaven is spread upon the earth but people do not see it."[20] Could he have been referring to the energy web? It is possible that these scriptures are teaching us the ways of working with consciousness and energy, and that the kingdom of heaven is the energy web where everything exists as a possibility.

Buddhists also view our reality in a quantum way. They see everything as unfolding out of nothing and returning to nothing. All is from one source. Everything is transient and in the process of becoming something else. There is a Buddhist chant that has been intoned in monasteries for hundreds of years: "The whole universe is an ocean of dazzling light and on it dance the waves of life and death."[21] We are beings of consciousness and energy dancing in this extraordinary universe we call home. With quantum understanding might we dance this precious life of ours with more skill and awareness? What is possible for us if we awaken to the deeper truths of our being, and what exactly are these deeper truths?

A reoccurring theme resonates throughout spirituality and quantum physics, revealing the same truth: there is no separation between us and everything else that exists in the universe. We are all one, and it is a oneness that matches the teachings of Buddha, Jesus, Einstein and the quantum gang of Bohr, Bohm and Heisenberg, to name but a few of the pioneering scientists who have revealed these truths to us.[22] Science and mysticism, while distrustful and antagonistic towards each another for hundreds of years, now amazingly find themselves joined together, saying the same thing, even if they are not always aware of it. We are all one.

It is a paradigm shift for us to move from the separateness and individuality that we know so well into merging with the wholeness of everything, but this is what we can do if we choose. It is the fine balancing act of living in two worlds simultaneously. In Japanese Buddhism the world of separate manifestations is referred to as *ji hokkai*, "the universe of things," and the unbounded, unified world as *ri hokkai*, "the absolute universe." These are the two different ways of experiencing our life. We can choose to see ourselves as an individual person, separate and distinct from others, or as an energy system immersed within the energy web and one with it. Both are accurate representations of our life. The way of the quantum warrior is to embrace both visions, since both are what in fact is happening to us, and to use whichever one suits our purpose at any given moment of time.

This duality of our reality is a paradox, a Zen koan,[23] a mystery to be contemplated, stretching our minds so that eventually we contain the extraordinary vastness and complexity of who we are. This can be done, must be done if we are to work effectively in these dimensions. By doing this we can change how we see ourselves and how we interact with the world.

Unlimited possibilities exist for us in quantum reality, so it is to our advantage to learn to navigate this frequency domain and access the vastness of its power. The more we tap into both frequencies, the more we develop quantum abilities. These are the steps that lead not only to greater understanding and personal power, but eventually to cosmic consciousness. As we practice quantum techniques we rewire the circuitry of our brain, change our neurology and become new beings.[24] Cosmic consciousness does not birth itself in full form all at once, but by gradual shifts of awareness, where one insight leads to another and one step builds upon another until a shift happens. This is the great work of conscious evolution.

The fields of depth psychology, physics and spirituality are filled with creative activity as new theories emerge. Trying to keep pace with the evolving and ever-changing landscape of what is being discovered is not always easy. Each of these fields is rich with new discoveries, theories, and of course controversies. This is a period of exceptional creativity and at the same time chaos and even revolution, where old paradigm models are under pressure everywhere. It sometimes seems bewildering as we wrestle with all this new information, but this is the necessary process in order to sweep out the old and bring in the new.

Einstein said, "A human being is part of the whole, called by us the universe. He experiences his thoughts and feelings as something separate from the rest . . . this a kind of optical delusion of his consciousness."[25] Fortunately this delusion of consciousness is now slowly but surely being replaced with a fresh new vision of who we are and how our species is evolving.

Participating in the world of quantum reality in a conscious systematic way is something different from anything we've ever experienced before. Actually, we have always been part of quantum reality; it's just that we've never been aware of it, so we have been unable to navigate within it or work with its power. This is about to change. We have the opportunity to become quantum warriors, to not just understand but to actually live the truths that science is revealing. Following this path unlocks extraordinary opportunities for us and, as we will discover, propels us into cosmic consciousness.

FOUR

The Mythology of a Quantum Warrior

"The world is unfathomable. And so are we,
and so is every being that exists in this world."
{ Carlos Castaneda }

To further explore the mystery of ourselves and our place in the universe, we now enter into the world of mythology. It may seem strange to suddenly shift from a scientific approach to discussing the merits of mythology, but it makes perfect sense from a psychological point of view. While science can help us understand the make-up of the universe and the mechanism of the brain, it struggles with consciousness, and here mythology can step in to fill the void in a unique way.

The mythic role we choose to embrace is that of *the quantum warrior*, with all the possibilities this choice brings us. It may appear to be an unusual path, but when we enter upon it we quickly see the wisdom of living our life this way. The term quantum warrior is a metaphor for what is possible in our life, and around this metaphor we build an elaborate mythology based upon the truths that quantum reality reveals to us. Viewing ourselves as the hero or heroine in our own personal life adventure enlivens us in ways nothing else can.

A well-designed mythology is a powerful tool which, when used skilfully, produces extraordinary results for the person possessing it. Respected author and psychologist James Hillman understood this well when he shared this little known fact: "Myths talk to the psyche in its own language; they speak emotionally, dramatically, sensuously, fantastically."[1] The psyche, we discover, responds well to mythic images because these images draw directly from the collective unconscious, holding deep meaning beyond what we would normally expect. Mythic symbols transcend logic and the rational mind, and in so doing open up ways for us to see and understand ourselves from a different perspective. When we employ the language of the fantastic in our own lives, thinking and acting in mythic ways, we align ourselves with the archetypical forces of the universe, and untold possibilities open up for us.

Mythic images uplift and inspire us to greatness for the simple reason that they are closer to the ultimate truth of who we are than the limited, constrictive images that our present-day culture has saddled us with. We need to free ourselves from the limited models we presently hold and become warriors, performing heroic acts, embarking upon great journeys, living our life fully. These opportunities exist for us when we live mythically.

The mythology of the quantum warrior has its roots in the quantum laws. Studying these laws we quickly realize what is possible when we embrace these truths and live in quantum ways. It is the vision of what is possible which compels us to live as quantum warriors, for above all else we desire to live fully and become all that we can. Our warrior journey is a quest to explore the mystery of ourselves, and in doing so the mysteries of the universe are revealed to us.

The word warrior conjures up many different associations, but within the context of this system, it simply means to be the best we can be in every situation. It means a dedication to excellence and authenticity in everything we do. There is a Tibetan word for warrior which comes from the word *pawo,* meaning "one who is brave."[2] This is a good description of what we can become when we train and discipline ourselves; we become brave. We are comfortable with who we are. We feel well equipped and competent to handle whatever comes our way. There is no arrogance in this feeling of competence; rather there is a deep understanding of ourselves and the world in which we live. As warriors our confidence is based upon our understanding and faith in the laws of the universe. We know that we are part of something greater than ourselves, and its power, we have discovered, is our power too. It is our connection with the universe that allows us to call upon warrior energy at any time, and to use it in the various areas of our life.

Warrior energy is nothing mysterious; all cultures have tapped into this source in one way or another. It is focused, dynamic energy directed towards a specific purpose. Men, women, young, old, we all use warrior energy, even if we do not always call it this. It is warrior energy that gets the exhausted mother up in the morning to feed her children and get them off to school. It is warrior energy that drives the entrepreneur to search for new ways of expanding his business, the athlete to train long and arduously so that she can perform at her best, the unemployed to send out résumés and follow more leads as he searches for work, the mystic to strive for enlightenment. Whatever life situations we find ourselves in, they can all be enhanced by calling upon warrior energy.

But we are not just ordinary warriors; we are quantum warriors, and this has deeper and more profound implications to it. As quantum warriors nothing is impossible for us. We are one with everything, and it is with this knowledge that we approach the countless experiences that present themselves to us. Each day becomes an opportunity for us to live in an extraordinary way, expanding who we are. Each day is part of our unique journey, and nothing is mundane or boring, since every circumstance we encounter is filled with possibility.

BECOMING A HUMAN BEING

Our first task as a quantum warrior is to learn how to become a human being. We have forgotten how to do this. Becoming a human being means becoming integrated and whole, and this requires that we come into relationship with our four 'energetic' parts: our mind, body, subconscious and soul. Each of these parts must be functioning and in relationship with each other part before we can call ourselves a complete human being. Until this happens we will only be a partial self, and there will be no harmony in our inner kingdom, for we will not know who we are and our different parts will be at war with one another. Becoming a complete and whole human being is not as easy as we might assume, mainly because we live most of our lives in our mind. It takes determination and effort to free ourselves from this habit. That we live most of our lives in our mind is a psychological truth we must face in order to rediscover who we are.

The saying "The whole is greater than the sum of the parts" has never been more appropriate than in describing our present situation as human beings. We are a cosmic organism designed to have all four of our parts functioning together as an ensemble. Until this happens we will live incomplete lives, never knowing ourselves. This is why becoming a human being is our first priority, for everything in our life depends upon us getting this right.

This journey of becoming a complete human being is a metamorphosis as transformative as the caterpillar becoming the butterfly. Not only will we become complete by integrating all parts of ourselves, we will become unrecognizable. Through this process we will awaken ourselves and discover who we are in the universe.

The term *awakened* means shifting our normal consciousness into something far greater. Different traditions use different names for this remarkable transition. In Christian terminology it is called being born again in the spirit, Buddhists call it enlightenment, evolutionists call it cosmic consciousness, and we as quantum warriors call it awakening. Regardless of what it is called, something extraordinary takes place when this shift occurs, and once it is achieved we are free to do or be whatever we choose; all eternity is ours to explore. This sounds incredible, but only because we have forgotten who we are and why we are here. We have lost our connection to the universe, and so the mystery and purpose of our life is hidden from us. We have not yet discovered that we are remarkable beings of consciousness and energy, seeded with cosmic possibilities awaiting our discovery of them.

Our modern culture has mostly forgotten that this is an epic journey, this being a human being. We have become too bogged down with the details of our life. We have become distracted, concerned with the wrong things. As the poet Ezra Pound said, "Man is concerned with man and forgets the whole and the flowing."[3] It is the whole and flowing that is too often missing in our lives. We have lost our feeling of connection to the universe, and even the connection to the different parts of ourselves. This is why the daily struggles of life often overwhelm us. How could they not? We need to change this way of living and understand the vastness of ourselves. We need to awaken.

The thirteenth-century Zen master Dōgen referred to this shift as "realization."[4] The Japanese word for realization means proof, evidence, witnessing. It is 'making real' that which was otherwise just a concept. Realization of who we are happens when the mythology of the quantum warrior becomes a lived reality. Our warrior mythology is not something we keep in our mind as a concept, taking it out and examining it like some manuscript or piece of art whenever we feel like it; rather it becomes something we bring into the world by living it. Author Heinrich Zimmer described it this way, "It is in doing that one becomes transformed. Executing a symbolic gesture, actually living through to the very limit a particular role, one comes to realize the truth inherent in the role."[5] Quantum warriorship gives us this opportunity.

To see our life as a mythic journey with meaning, purpose and wonder is to give it meaning, purpose and wonder. To see our life as dull and meaningless is to make it dull and meaningless. There are some who see themselves as failures, inadequate, having nothing to offer the world. They see their life as filled with hardships, and these descriptions weave themselves within their psyche and hold them captive, under a spell of their own conjuring. All of us are held captive in one way or another by our beliefs. As warriors we understand how this works, for we understand consciousness and are only too aware of the ways we can trip ourselves up. This is why we are disciplined, vigilant and dedicated to the vision of awakening. We never forget who we are and why we are here.

The symbol of the quantum warrior, when built regularly within our psyche, assists us to connect with mystic mythologies that have existed from the beginning and which reside within the collective unconscious. These mythologies, based upon past cultures and practices, have at their core noble ideals. To have a strong moral code, a work ethic that cuts through laziness and indifference, the ability to sacrifice ourselves to something greater than ourselves, to help those less fortunate, to follow our destiny, all are possibilities that quantum warriorship offers us.

Some think that a mythology is something untrue, a fable, a fairy tale, something we make up. This is not what mythologies are at all. The mind requires inventory and so has already created an elaborate mythology for us. Each of us carries within us a personal inner mythology, whether we are aware of it or not. Probably it has been constructed unconsciously; most of our mythologies are. Given that they are unconscious, you could say these mythologies live us, rather than the other way around. A deeply held belief, neurosis, obsession or ideal has a power of its own for both good and bad. We human beings naturally create mythologies for ourselves, even if we've never thought of it in this way. A Christian has his mythology, as does a Buddhist, and an atheist too for that matter. Each in their own way interprets the universe and comes to conclusions about themselves and the purpose and meaning of their lives. Motherhood and fatherhood carry with them mythologies, sets of duties and obligations real and imagined that we create and project upon ourselves. We define ourselves in many different ways, and each definition carries a mythology with it. Our mind requires a model of reality to function, so it is not that we don't have mythologies within us already; it is just that our present models are far less than they could be.

Our warrior mythology is a way of enhancing our life. It is our gift to the world. We call upon ourselves to be the best we can be in every situation, to become a complete human being, to awaken. This is what we expect of ourselves, and to this vision we are devoted.

THE MONOPOLY AND COSMIC GAMES

As warriors we learn that there are only two games we get to play in life: the cosmic game and the monopoly game. Every activity that makes up our life can be divided into one of these two games. Monopoly is the first game we play as human beings, and it begins from the moment we are born. Gathering inventory is part of playing monopoly, so too is learning to speak, going to school, having our first boyfriend or girlfriend. It's all monopoly. Choosing careers, getting married, making money, raising children, travelling the world, saving for retirement, going to concerts, building a business; again, all more of the monopoly game. The monopoly game is everything we do to create a meaningful and successful life. It is a game of accumulation, of achieving goals, and it is a worthy game for a human being to play. It is challenging, exciting, filled with extraordinary experiences. When we are succeeding it is exhilarating, but when hardships or failures occur it can be frightening, numbing, terrifying. But these too are built-in parts of the game. All experiences good and bad, pleasant and unpleasant serve their purpose in a warrior's life, for they are all part of our game unfolding, and as such they have meaning for us.

I love the monopoly game. My original mind power training was specifically designed to assist me in playing monopoly, and I have played the game well, but it is not the only game we get to play in life. There is a second game, a mysterious, secret game we get to play—if we are fortunate enough to discover it. This second game is the cosmic game. The goal of the cosmic game is to awaken ourselves. It is a warrior game, and once the opportunities and nuances of this game are understood it takes up more and more of our attention. When we play the cosmic game we are playing for different stakes, and on a much larger scale. In the cosmic game we play not just in time and space, but in the quantum dimensions, and we play for all of eternity.

Describing our life as comprised of the cosmic and monopoly games allows us to approach it with a different attitude. Not surprisingly, by making it all a game we can relax and find the rhythm and flow of every situation. There is a real advantage to living our life this way. When life becomes a game it makes it more enjoyable and opens up new creative possibilities. We now realize there is no reason to be worked up or concerned about every detail, no matter how large or small the challenges we face. This perspective takes the pressure off everything. We can simply focus on being our best in every situation, which is exactly what we should be doing in the first place. There are many tricks that a warrior learns in order to be effective in life and this is one of them. We take all pressure off ourselves. All that is ever required of us is to be our best, and when we do this we can relax, knowing we have fulfilled our duty. We can let "the ten thousand things" unfold as they may. The term "the ten thousand things" is a metaphor, one of the ways we describe our life unfolding. Actually, there are three terms quantum warriors use which are interchangeable: the game, our life journey, the ten thousand things. As they are slightly different metaphors they elicit slightly different responses from our subconscious, and this is why we use all three. These terms become part of our warrior vocabulary.

Warrior mythology is a way of living with daily routines and practices. This powerful mythology, once established in our consciousness, is extremely advantageous. It allows us to focus our attention on what is really important, to not get sidetracked by pettiness, fear or doubt. As warriors our life is simple. Our path is crystal clear. We know we are called to become a human being, awaken ourselves and be our best in every situation. This is all that is required. Where this leads us is unknown, but with this clarity as our compass our journey has begun, and ten thousand adventures lie before us.

Psychologist David Feinstein describes living mythically this way: "To live mythically is to seek guidance from our dreams, imagination and other reflections of our inner being, as well as from the most inspiring people, practices, and institutions of our society. To live mythically is to cultivate an ever-deepening relationship with the universe and its great mysteries."[6]

Our quantum warrior mythology, when embraced as a discipline, becomes our companion, and with it we transform ourselves into something greater than we could ever attain on our own. Our present-day culture has forgotten this method, and instead has elevated logical, rational thinking to such a dominant position that such thinking has become neurotic, counterproductive and stifling to our spirits. Our psyche hungers to break free from these restraints and roam the wild open fields of the fantastic. Ironically, by living mythically we bring some sanity back into our lives.

Throughout this book the mythic image of the quantum warrior will be used for the simple reason that it has great power. If you, on the other hand, choose to exchange this term with another, perhaps athlete of the mind, or any other image that seems more appropriate for you, you have this choice. Choice is a warrior tool and we must use it skilfully in everything we do. The key is to find something that will uplift us, shake us out of our present model of reality and awaken our quantum possibilities. Everything else is just detail, and we must know this absolutely or else we will get lost in a maze of our own creation. Mythology is a tool, no more or no less, but it is a powerful tool and used skilfully will open doors for us that are unavailable through any other means. As warriors everything we do has meaning, and embracing and living our quantum warrior mythology is no exception. With this mythology well established within us everything becomes possible.

FIVE

Beliefs

"Whatever the mind of man can conceive
and believe it can achieve."
{ Napoleon Hill }

From a psychological perspective our beliefs are personal inventory which make up our model of reality. From a quantum perspective our beliefs are vibrating energy patterns within our own personal quantum field. However, from a warrior perspective, beliefs are a creative act of choice. They are the most powerful tools we possess.

Our beliefs are the single most important factor in determining what will happen to us, yet most of us pay them minimal if any attention. This must change if we wish to play monopoly and cosmic successfully. Beliefs are not phantom or shadow images without substance; they are patterns of energy vibrating within us. Quantum warriors call beliefs "laws of power," as they resonate their vibrational message throughout the entire energy web, attracting the people, circumstances and events that match these energy vibrations. This is why we pay them so much attention.

Beliefs have an uncanny way of becoming self-fulfilling, and from a quantum perspective you would expect this to happen. Until now we have mostly chosen our beliefs unconsciously, in that we are often unaware of how or even when they came into being. This is going to change. As our quantum awareness increases we realize that we are free to believe whatever we choose. This opens up a whole new way of 'playing the game.' Now we can be much more creative and daring with our beliefs.

'Inner programs' is another way of describing beliefs, which leads us to the obvious analogy of the brain functioning like a computer. The brain and the computer do indeed operate in a similar fashion, and it is good for us to know this. We know that with our computer we can only work with the programs that have been installed in it. We might want to work with Photoshop, but if we haven't installed it we can't work with it. The same applies with consciousness. We may want to have a prosperity consciousness,[1] but if we haven't installed it within us, we can't just call upon it at will. To work with prosperity consciousness, or, to be more exact, to have it working for us, it must first be installed. The same applies with a success consciousness or a health consciousness; if we wish to have these programs functioning within us, they must be installed.

TAKING INVENTORY

Beliefs are as necessary to the mind as our organs are to the body. Our mind cannot function without beliefs, so it creates them in order to interpret and make sense of what is happening in our life. We have many beliefs but now, understanding the power of these inner programs, we need to examine each of our beliefs to see whether they serve us or not. We call this process *taking inventory.*

We examine our beliefs about money, health, relationships; all areas of our life are scrutinized to discover what we are currently believing. Each belief must now have a purpose in our life; it must be supportive of what we are trying to achieve. We realize we cannot have scarcity beliefs and hope to be prosperous, or be fearful and negative and expect to be successful. To achieve success in any area of our life we must have empowering beliefs that support us. Our beliefs are forever at work in our life. No belief is without its effect, and what we believe will most certainly influence what happens to us. As we sow, so shall we reap. This is a law of the universe, and we must be aware of how this law operates in our life.

An old-world fable illustrates this principle:

There was a wise old man sitting quietly by the main gate leading into an ancient city. A number of refugees fleeing a pestilence that had ravaged the country were coming to make their home in this new, unknown city. One traveller stopped at the gate to ask the old man, "What are the people like in this city?"

"What were the people like in the city you left?" the old man asked.

"Oh they were terrible. They robbed and cheated and lied and you couldn't trust anyone. You had to watch over your shoulder constantly. It was dreadful."

The old man nodded his head and said, "You'll find people here much the same." The stranger sighed in resignation and entered the gate with a heavy heart. Very shortly after this, another man arrived at the gate and asked the old man the same question, "What are the people like in this city?"

"What were the people like in the city you left?" asked the old man.

"Oh they were wonderful. Generous, loving, thoughtful; you could always count on someone to help you if you were in need."

"You'll find them much the same here," answered the old man, and the stranger entered the gate with a cheerful heart.

The message in this tale is clear. Each of the men would attract to themselves their own set of circumstances, according to the beliefs they held, so the wise man could accurately predict what would happen to them.

A Zen adage says, "Wherever you go—there you are." We take our energy and vibration with us everywhere we go, and not much will change in our life until this does. We are beings of consciousness and energy, and who we are resonates as a distinct vibration throughout the energy web. It is our energy signature; this is how the universe knows us.

FOUNDATION BELIEFS

Teaching mind power for over thirty years has given me the unique opportunity of sharing these methods with numerous people, observing firsthand how these people either accept or resist working with them. The idea that we can simply change our beliefs whenever we choose is radical to most people.

Whenever I'm working with someone who has a major goal they wish to achieve, I always start with foundation beliefs. I ask the person, "What are your core foundation beliefs?" If this person has not worked with me before or never been exposed to my teaching, they will most likely draw a blank. Most people are unaware of what beliefs they hold, much less what their foundation beliefs are, but there are ways of discovering them. As a starter we can notice what our mind thinks about on a day-to-day basis. This is an extremely valuable practice revealing a lot about our inner programs.

Cindy, a woman whom I worked with several years ago, wanted a relationship desperately. She was in her midthirties, wanted children and felt ready to make a commitment. Her goal was very clear: to be in a meaningful relationship within a year, but by observing her thoughts she discovered that she had many limiting beliefs about relationships. She discovered that she was thinking things like, "All the good men are already taken, and those remaining have problems," and "So many of my friends are divorcing; relationships don't last," and "I'm not as attractive as I used to be." (Translated: "I'm no longer attractive.") These were her thoughts about relationships, revealing to her, her foundation beliefs. These were the messages she was vibrating into the web.

Cindy's foundation beliefs were in direct conflict with what she wanted to happen. This is more common than you would suspect; in fact, I would go so far as to say it is probably the single biggest reason why most people don't achieve their goals. No one will ever achieve a goal when their foundation beliefs are contradictory to what they desire. I pointed this out to Cindy. "But this is what is happening in my life," she argued, "I can't force myself to believe something that is not true."

I hear this a lot. We are reluctant to change our beliefs, even when they are holding us back. We become entrenched in our positions, making excuses for being stuck in situations we don't like. We have yet to understand how we can dramatically change our present situation by simply changing our beliefs. Our subconscious is designed to accept whatever beliefs we give to it. It was created for the specific purpose of taking instructions from us. Our subconscious mind is our secret partner in success, yet we have never been shown how to use it. The fact is we can train our mind to think whatever we want. We can substitute new, empowering beliefs for limiting ones any time we choose. This is a warrior skill we develop. As we master the skill of choosing empowering beliefs our life changes dramatically, and everything becomes possible for us.

Explaining this to Cindy, she suddenly saw her situation differently; she realized she needed to change her beliefs if she hoped to be successful in attracting a relationship. Her belief that there were "no good men available" was not helping her, and needed to be changed. Talking to her about it logically, we figured that in a city of over a million people, with half being men, her belief that there were "no good men" (her exact words) was a ridiculous exaggeration that her subconscious had accepted and was presently working with. We decided a very conservative estimate was that there would be thousands, if not tens of thousands of available single men in the city who she would be very happy with. She accepted this as a theoretical possibility, though her mind still remained doubtful, for she had been dating unsuccessfully for many years. However, she understood the concept of having this belief operating for her, so she imprinted this new supportive belief, as well as others, into her subconscious in ways I will share with you shortly. Not surprisingly, as she changed her beliefs she shifted her energy and things began changing quickly for her. Within months she was meeting new and interesting people, and four months after beginning this practice she met someone, fell in love and they are now happily married.

I have witnessed dramatic changes in thousands of my students when they take the initiative in changing their beliefs. When we change our beliefs we change the vibration in our personal quantum field. New beliefs change our energy signature; they change who we are.

We've all heard the saying, "I'll believe it when I see it." But this is totally backwards. Why would we wait till we see something before we believe it? We might never see it. Better to believe it first, let the belief become an active force within us, and then we attract 'it' to us. Our new quantum mantra becomes, "I'll see it when I believe it." Sounds radical? It is radical, but this is exactly what Jesus advises us to do. Jesus speaks of beliefs in a very specific way, a quantum way: "And all things, whatsoever ye shall ask in prayer, believing, ye shall receive."[2] Now notice the interesting change of tense in this scripture, for this is the key to understanding its meaning. We have to believe it first. We are advised to actually believe something that isn't real before we will receive it. The belief comes first. Radical as a concept, but it works because it is in alignment with the known laws of the universe. Jesus understood and worked with the energy web thousands of years before scientists revealed the quantum reality.

If the universe was operating according to the Newtonian model of reality we would not be able to do this. We could conceive of how beliefs might help our confidence and motivate us, but not much more than that, for whatever was going to happen would happen regardless of what we believed. This is how the old Newtonian model explained our reality. According to this outdated theory, our thoughts and beliefs have no bearing on what is going to happen to us. The quantum model, however, presents something entirely different to us. The quantum model informs us that our beliefs are constantly shaping and creating our reality. These are totally different interpretations of how life works, and we know which model is real. You do know which one is real, don't you? I ask this because even though we conceptually know what is true we still, too often, live and act as if the Newtonian model was the one operating in our life. Many of us still haven't made the shift into living in a quantum way. We still view ourselves as separate from everything else, clinging to the Newtonian model of reality even though science is telling us this is not what is happening. We just can't seem to get over the hurdle where our senses are telling us one thing and science something else. We trust the reality we see rather than the invisible energy web of oneness, and in doing so we have bought fool's gold.

Foundation beliefs are, as their name suggests, the foundation, the premise from which we think and act and make our choices. If we have a goal of earning a million dollars, winning a major sporting event, or healing ourselves of an illness, having foundation beliefs that support this goal is essential. For example, trying to be successful financially while believing that the odds are stacked against us, that it probably won't happen, no matter what we do, will not attract the results we want. We can employ our various mind power techniques, and they will make us feel more confident, but if at our core we are vibrating the wrong messages, this is what will ultimately make the difference. Financial success requires we have foundation beliefs that will attract this kind of success to us. We might choose foundation beliefs such as, "There are many opportunities for me to succeed," or "I have unique talents that will be well rewarded," or "I am neurologically wired for success." Vibrating these beliefs sets in motion energy patterns that attract the opportunities for our success.

Similarly, if we wish to heal ourselves and recover from an illness, we must have strong foundation beliefs about health and healing resonating within us. We don't want to simply hope for the best and wait to see what happens, and we absolutely don't want to worry that we won't get better. We want foundation beliefs that promote health resonating within us day and night. Foundation beliefs such as, "The body is a healing organism," or "I am connected to the energy web and it is healing me through my intention," or "I have a strong immune system," or "I always heal quickly," or "Every day in every way I'm getting better and better"; these are foundation beliefs that, vibrating within the web on our behalf, will keep us healthy. And once these beliefs are established within us, we don't even have to think them; they think us. That is the beauty of foundation beliefs; once established they work day and night for us.

THE PLACEBO EFFECT

The placebo effect is one of the most fascinating aspects of our reality, something that still stretches our ideas about what is possible. It is as controversial today as it was almost sixty years ago when it was first discovered. Traditional medicine, while aware of the placebo effect, still does not know quite what to do with it. Many advocates of placebo use see it as a cure-all for everything. Its opponents call it a sham, an illusion exposing patients to unnecessary risks and building up false hope. What both sides agree on, however, is that in many cases placebos work. Now new research is indicating that its success is far wider and more encompassing than originally suspected.[3]

Placebos first came to the general public's attention in the 1950s. It was discovered that patients who were given harmless sugar pills and told they were medicine would often report themselves cured. In an influential article first published in 1955, Harvard researcher Henry Beecher concluded that between thirty and forty percent of any treated group would respond to a placebo.[4] Now, half a century later, after countless experiments, we are finding that the success rate is still as high today as when first discovered, often exceeding the results of prescribed medications. Remarkably, it's not unheard of for the success of the placebo effect to exceed that of the normally prescribed treatment. The implications of this are staggering.

Take, for example, the experiment conducted by surgeon Bruce Moseley in the summer of 1994. Moseley had ten patients scheduled for an operation intended to relieve arthritis pain in their knees. The patients, all men and military veterans, were wheeled into an operating room at the Houston Veterans Affairs Medical Center. All ten were draped, examined and anaesthetized. All ten were dispatched the next day with crutches and a painkiller. What happened while they were under anaesthesia, however, differed greatly. Two of them underwent the standard arthroscopic surgery, three had a rinsing alone, and five had no surgical procedure at all. Moseley simply stabbed the knees of these five patients three times with a scalpel to provide the appearance of surgery. I should add at this point that all ten patients were aware that they were part of a unique experiment; however, they did not know who would receive the real surgery and who would not. Neither did Moseley, since he recognized that if he knew in advance what he was going to do with each patient he might inadvertently indicate as much to the patient. It wasn't until he was actually in the operating room and the patient was anaesthetized that he opened an envelope telling him whether he was doing a genuine procedure or a fake one. All three groups went through postoperative care which included an exercise program.[5]

The placebo treatment worked. Six months after surgery, still unaware of whether they had genuine surgery or not, all ten reported much less pain. All were happy with the outcome of the operation. One of the patients who had been assigned to the placebo group, a seventy-six-year-old from Beaumont, Texas, was interviewed several years after the experiment. He was by then mowing his lawn regularly and walking whenever he wanted to. "The surgery was two years ago," he reported, "and the knee has never bothered me since. It's just like my other knee now. I give a whole lot of credit to Dr. Moseley."

Another member of the placebo group, Tim Perez, who had to walk with a cane before the surgery, now plays basketball with his grandchildren. All the patients who had received the placebo surgery were told after two years what had actually happened, but by then the results had been accepted by the mind and the body. There was no turning back. Perez summed up his experience this way, "In this world anything is possible when you put your mind to it. I know that your mind can work miracles."

These discoveries have given birth to a whole new area of investigation, "placebo surgery." It seems the merely 'symbolic' acts of surgery—the shedding of blood, the perceived knowledge and wisdom of the surgeons, even the scars that focus the mind on the 'dramatic' act—these are all a critical part of the healing process.

In fact, if you examine the medical practices that have been used in centuries past, traditional western medicine has consisted almost entirely of the placebo effect, with elaborate sideshows for effect. Neither the patients nor the doctors realized at the time that they were performing useless, even harmful acts, but how else would you describe bleeding, leeching, or some of the other bizarre treatments and potions administered in the name of medicine in days past? In most cases patients got better in spite of the treatment, not because of it. The doctors who administered what we now know was hocus-pocus treatment believed in what they were doing, and the patients trusted and believed in their doctors. There was belief from both sides, and now that we understand how belief plays such an important part in healing—some might argue the most important part—we can understand how these practices produced results. Few if any of the healing methods used in the nineteenth century are used today, and yet they worked at the time.

But the potential benefits of placebo beliefs are far greater than just healing the body. Since placebos work so well in healing, might they work equally well in other areas of our life? Could we perhaps use placebo beliefs to make more money, attract a meaningful relationship, play a better game of golf, become enlightened? Could we make ourselves lucky, for example, using a placebo belief? Well, that's exactly what I did twenty years ago.

It happened over a period of six months while I was sailing with my friend Jim Burns in our sailboat, the Akimbo. It seemed that almost every time we took our boat out for a sail it would be good weather. Now this was in the Pacific Northwest, where it rains a lot and can be sunny one hour and raining the next, but we kept enjoying consistently good weather, and each time I would say to Jim, "Just our luck." It was said in fun, and yet I was also aware that by saying this, even in fun, I was programming my mind each time I repeated this statement. It became my summer mantra and I would say it many times. We had an extraordinary season of fabulous weather, which allowed me to use the affirmation a lot.

But it didn't stop with just the weather. I got into the habit of saying, "Just my luck," every time something good would happen to me. It was not lost on me that I was turning a well-known expression on its head. Think about how many times you've heard someone say, "Just my luck." What were they referring to? They were always commenting on some misfortune that had happened to them. Have you ever heard someone use this expression in a positive way? That's what I chose to do.

"Just my luck" started out as little more than a fun comment, but then I noticed that I was getting lucky in other areas of my life as well. I was at a charity art event and guess who won the painting? I tried to buy tickets to a sold-out Leonard Cohen concert, and while I was on the phone to Ticketmaster the operator was explaining to me how the concert had been sold out for weeks, when suddenly she paused and said, "Oh, wait. This is unusual; we just have two tickets that have come available. They're in the third row." I booked them. "You're very lucky," she said. "I know," I replied. Hanging up the phone I repeated to myself, "Just my luck." By now I was very conscious of what this practice was doing for me. My brother Tom organized a hockey event for our family, booking a private box for a game, and I flew to Toronto to be there. The arena was packed with twenty thousand hockey fans. Guess who won the 50/50 draw that night, taking home almost ten thousand dollars? There are numerous other examples I could share, and now the reality of my life is that I am consistently very lucky, with fortuitous events happening to me regularly. Not that I was unlucky before, but my luck wasn't anything like it is now. Does it surprise me that this is happening? Not at all; I expect it. It has become part of my model of reality.

Over a century ago, philosopher and psychologist William James expressed an insight that is so simple yet so profound that it changes how we view ourselves: "A new life is but a new mind." The truth of our reality is that each of us is free to believe whatever we choose, and whatever beliefs we choose become resonating laws of power within us. With this insight warriors build themselves unique models of reality, using powerful foundation beliefs. We do it because we understand what these beliefs will do for us. The following four quantum maxims are the foundation of our warrior model of reality and become integral parts of our mythology.

FOUNDATION BELIEFS OF A QUANTUM WARRIOR

1. The consciousness that created the universe dwells within us.

Our mind is a tiny holographic piece of the consciousness that pervades the universe. While our mind is mostly preoccupied with its own little sphere of self, it is nonetheless part of the great cosmic mind, with access to everything contained within that cosmos. While controversial, this is not an unreasonable concept, as it is supported by the facts that quantum theory reveals. We take on this belief because we have the ability to do so through choice. This belief is further backed by the vision revealed to us by the great mystics of our race, and now viewing ourselves differently we accept their truth as ours. It is also not lost on us the advantage that having such a belief will have in our life. Think about it; if the consciousness that created a universe is in us, what can it not do in our life? What problems or challenges are too great for us now that we know this consciousness is in us? With this belief, suddenly everything becomes possible for us.

2. We exist in the energy web and are one with it.

All things come from the unmanifest and will return to the unmanifest. The unmanifest is that which is not, or, to be more exact, that which is not yet. It is the creative force of the energy web. It is the first cause from which all things in the universe of time and space are created. We are all children of this unmanifest. All things—galaxies, ants, oceans, human beings—all are birthed from the same source. We are part of the whole and one with it. All things are our brothers and sisters—people, plants, animals, even time and space; we are in relationship with all things.

3.   Consciousness weaves and directs energy.

The energy web responds to our instructions and acts upon them. It is designed to be responsive to consciousness. The web exists in a perpetual state of unlimited potential awaiting consciousness to act upon it. Everything in the world of ten thousand things has its own unique vibration, its energy signature, including ourselves. Our communication with the web is through vibrational messages. Each thought and belief we hold communicates with the energy web via its unique vibrational signature. The language of the universe is vibrating energy. As we learn to communicate in the mysterious language of the universe we learn the secrets of working with the energy web.

4.   Everything exists for us as a possibility.

There are no limitations other than those we impose upon ourselves. Everything is possible for those who believe. The universe is greater and more mysterious than we could ever imagine. It exists in a state of continuous possibility, and we are one with it. We believe in our ability to do or become anything because we believe in a universe of unlimited possibilities.

While cloaked in mythic references, these four beliefs are backed by quantum theory. It is possible for us to believe these quantum maxims and live them as our truths. We imprint these quantum maxims into our subconscious where they become our laws of power, and with these laws we have the means to perform great acts.

IMPRINTING BELIEFS

Now let me reveal the secrets of imprinting beliefs into our subconscious. What is 6 times 6? Here's another, 9 times 8? How is it that we know these answers instantly, quicker than we can punch the numbers into a calculator? It is because we have imprinted the multiplication tables into our consciousness through numerous repetitions. Think back to when you were in school. Think of how many times these tables were repeated, written and spoken. So many times that now they are firmly imprinted. We need not practice them ever again, or refresh ourselves—they are programmed within us.

The exact same method used to imprint the multiplication tables can be used to imprint new beliefs directly into our subconscious. We do this through repetition and daily practice. For five minutes a day we concentrate our attention as vividly as possible upon whatever belief we wish to imprint. For example, we can imprint the quantum maxim, "Consciousness weaves and directs energy." Using the imprinting technique we focus for five minutes each day on this statement. We repeat to ourselves, "Consciousness weaves and directs energy," then we let our mind consider the implications of this. When our mind drifts to other matters, we bring our attention back to the statement, restate it once again, "Consciousness weaves and directs energy," and refocus. We feel the power and implication of what we are saying. We repeat this process over and over again to ourselves, affirming to ourselves this statement, allowing our mind to absorb the significance. We close our mind off to all other thoughts, focusing solely upon the statement. The repetition, whether verbal or mental, is important because it is only through repetition that we activate new neurological circuits. We claim the truth of this statement absolutely, focusing as completely as we can on this statement, letting it vibrate within us. We let the words energize us. When the exercise is completed, we allow our mind to think about whatever it wants to, until the next day when we repeat the exercise. Through this process, what was originally just an interesting concept begins to come alive for us as it takes hold in our subconscious.

I remember clearly the first time I used the imprinting technique. It was while I was living in my cabin in British Columbia. I was still experimenting with these methods and had begun a daily program to imprint the belief, "I have unlimited power at my disposal." This was something I wanted to believe, so each day I would affirm to myself, "I have unlimited power at my disposal." I would contemplate how I was connected to the energy web, how thoughts are real forces, that I had access to this unlimited power any time I chose. I would direct my mind to think about these things. I disciplined myself to follow this routine for five minutes each day. Five minutes doesn't sound like much time, but we now know that intensely focusing our thoughts for short intervals produces neurological changes. A five-minute exercise practiced daily over a period of months produces extraordinary results.

Now some days when I finished my exercise I felt inspired, feeling the powerful truth of what I was saying to myself. Other days, however, the process felt cold and mechanical, and although I was saying the words and contemplating their meaning they just didn't seem real to me. It was almost like I was lying to myself. Adding to this, my mind would sometimes say things to me like, "Unlimited power? Ha. You're broke; you have nothing happening in your life. You're a loser." All I could do was ignore these thoughts and carry on. So some days, during the exercise, it felt real and powerful and some days cold and mechanical, but here is the important point I want to emphasize. *I did it every day, whether I felt like it or not.* Regardless of whether I was inspired or not, I did it every day. It was a discipline I had committed to.

I will never forget the moment I knew absolutely that this belief was imprinted in my subconscious as a vibrating law of power. It was several months after beginning the exercise. I woke up in the middle of the night alert, aware, with my mind ablaze with certainty that I actually did have "unlimited power at my disposal." I could feel the truth of this statement resonating within me. It was no longer a concept I wanted to believe; I now knew with absolute certainty that I did indeed have unlimited power at my disposal. And this feeling has never left me. It's a permanent part of my model of reality.

As warriors we have the privilege of choosing our beliefs. Our mythology of what is possible allows us to do this. This is a great advantage, for it gives us ways of weaving the web that most people do not understand. Choosing beliefs is a tool, and we use it skilfully. Once we realize what is possible for us we never go back to our old way of thinking. Having committed ourselves to be our best in every situation, we naturally take on the best, most empowering beliefs.

We learn to play monopoly with this new skill of choosing beliefs, and we discover that having empowering beliefs makes us more successful at the game. We train ourselves to believe that we will be successful, attract opportunities, have good fortune and vibrant health, and these beliefs help to create these things for us. Later we will use the same process to play cosmic, as we take on new more visionary beliefs for ourselves, and this too will create our reality. Choosing beliefs, we discover, is one of our most important skills, and like a master craftsman, in the privacy of our own mind we build our model of reality without anyone knowing what we are doing.

Not everyone sees the world the way we do or has our understanding of the power of beliefs; this we know. In our encounters with others, we quickly learn to keep our own counsel, to be private about these matters. While we discreetly design our own model of reality, accumulating our own beliefs, we allow each person to believe whatever they choose no matter how contrary that may be to our vision. We have no need to convince others of the validity of the positions we hold. We can allow different beliefs, different models of reality to exist without feeling threatened in our own truth. There is no need for others to agree with us. Each of us is different, and that's just the way it is. No two of us are the same. None of us have had the same experiences; nor do we have the same vision of what is possible, so how could we possibly believe the same things?

We are all weaving the energy web according to our own concepts, some of us aware of what we are doing and some of us not. Each of us is playing the game to the best of our abilities. All the while we are interconnecting with each other in the most intimate ways, as friends, family members, coworkers, lovers, strangers, adversaries, all of us living mythologies of our own creation. The game has been designed so that each of us plays it in our own unique way. There are no restrictions put upon us. We have unlimited creative freedom to believe whatever we choose.

SIX

Athletes of the Mind

"The master of any activity
is undoubtedly a master of practice."
{ George Leonard }

Quantum warriors are first and foremost athletes of the mind. We have a vision of what is possible and we know the ways by which we can achieve it. We understand that the key to our success is our ability to master and train our mind, and we dedicate ourselves to this task. Daily we train, increasing our understanding of the quantum laws, weaving energy, developing character, strengthening our will, sharpening our focus and imagination. Training in this way, we come to know ourselves and appreciate our unique place in the universe, where everything exists for us as a possibility.

A quantum warrior's training bears striking similarities to the way top professional athletes train to master their skills and achieve peak performance. I have long been interested in the training practices of athletes, and have had many close relationships with professional athletes and coaches at the highest level. The training similarities between top athletes and quantum warriors are too obvious to ignore. Both train regularly, are committed to excellence, have clearly defined goals and play to win. We can learn a great deal by studying the practices of elite athletes.

Performance coach Jim Murphy, author of *Inner Excellence*, knows well what is required to perform at the highest level of athletics. Jim has trained many professional and Olympian athletes to achieve their very best. He knows what is required to excel, and Jim and I have had many an occasion to compare the similarities between these two disciplines.

"Peak performance has a few common characteristics," Jim says. "The top athletes have three characteristics when they perform at their best: a clear mind, positive focused energy, and powerful beliefs."

"How and what they think is crucial. It is the core of a champion. Who they are, how they train and how they compete really come down to how they think. An athlete wanting to perform at his peak needs to develop powerful beliefs about him or herself. The elite athlete practices controlling his thoughts and feelings, developing a powerful focus, and becomes a presence in the process."[1]

Becoming "a presence" is an interesting choice of words, for they are the words warriors use in describing what happens when we train. When we train regularly and dedicate ourselves to a vision, something noticeable changes within us. We become our thoughts and beliefs. We become a presence.

Each of us is born with the neural wiring to be successful, but more is required to excel at the highest levels. If we wish to elevate ourselves to where we become athletes of the mind, another level of commitment is necessary. We must train to be our best, and as warriors we have committed ourselves to be our best. Training is not just our means to achieve success; it is our path to becoming a human being.

"One thing that helps is creating daily routines," Murphy explains. "The best athletes have routines in all areas of their lives, including the night before a game, on game day, pre-game, during the game and after the game. Over time they've created a 'recipe' for success that enables them to perform at their best, and they stick to the recipe. They have mental, physical and even spiritual routines, and this helps them focus their energy. When you have powerful beliefs and regular routines you will excel. The key is to practice."

TRAINING THE MIND

The key to a warrior's success is also practice. With powerful beliefs and regular routines we can achieve anything. However, before we even begin our training we must understand very clearly the unique role our mind plays in who we are. I want you to pay close attention to what I am about to say. The next sentence contains a key to understanding ourselves. *We are not our mind.* This is crucial to understand, for if we do not know this we are sure to be deceived in life. We have associated ourselves so completely with our mind that we have forgotten that we are much more than this thinking part of ourselves. Just as we are not our hands and feet—they are only parts of who we are—so too are we not our mind. Our mind is only a part of who we are. We need to remind ourselves many times of this distinction, or else we will be fooled and captured by our mind. For this reason I will refer to "us" and our "mind" as if they were different from one another, which in fact they are. It may sound strange to our ear, but making this distinction helps us understand the complexity of what we are. Distinguishing ourselves from our mind in this way facilitates a shift in how we think of ourselves, making us more effective in our training.

Our mind believes its only role is to think thoughts, and it does so in whatever way it chooses. When we let our mind function like this we are at the mercy of our mind. This is exactly the reverse of how we want our mind to work. Through exercises, we train our mind to work for us; we hold it responsible for the tasks we give it. We train it to think the specific thoughts we choose for it, and to listen to our instructions. We train the mind in the ways of warriorship.

Our conscious mind has three main functions. It is Custodian of the Will, Guardian to the Gates of the Subconscious and Weaver of the Patterns. These are not psychological terms that you will find in any textbook; these are mythic terms, charged with imagery representing psychological functions. We describe the mind's functions in this way because practice has proven that it is easier to assimilate mythic terms rather than cold technical terms. By describing the mind's functions in this way we educate the mind to its duties, and these titles reveal mysteries to us as we integrate them into our mythology.

As Custodian of the Will the mind has immense power over us, controlling what we think and do. Whoever controls the will has the power to control the self. Sometimes unconscious patterns can hijack the will, and this will be addressed in later chapters, but in normal circumstances it is the mind that decides what activities we pursue, how we live our life. What we believe has been decided for us by our mind. We have not constructed our model of reality through choice or vision, but rather our mind has created it for us according to its views and peculiarities. Because we think we are our mind, we have not even noticed how this has happened. Without warrior training we are destined to remain captive in our mind's model of reality, accepting its beliefs and following its instructions blindly. As custodian of the will the mind rules the self, and it is not always willing to give up this control. The mind, however, does not hold the will exclusively. It is only the custodian, and it is trained to be a wise custodian, using this power with discernment. Eventually, when we awaken, the other parts of the self will share the will with the mind, but this is a later stage.

There is an old maxim which says that the mind is a wonderful servant but a terrible master. This is very true, and so we take back our power through training the mind, assisting it to understand its rightful place in the evolving self. If this seems strange it is only because we have forgotten who we are.

The second mythic title of the mind is Guardian to the Gates of the Subconscious. When our mind is first introduced to this concept, which is really a job description, it is surprised to learn this, for it had no idea this was one of its functions, and how could it, for this is not commonly known. Until the mind understands what is required of it, it remains unaware of its role and place in the self. It does not know yet that, with training, it will become masterful, know great truths and understand the mysteries of the universe. The mind is designed for more than just thinking thoughts.

As we begin our training, the mind becomes excited about the possibilities this path holds for it, and this is good. We need our mind to be enthusiastic about its training; in this way it will cooperate with us. We lay out the advantages that training will bring the mind. This is the carrot we use to entice our mind to cooperate with us. The mind has an insatiable appetite to know and understand everything. We skilfully exploit this curiosity, convincing the mind to take on new tasks. Otherwise, being very set in its ways, it sees no reason to change. We win the mind over to this new system and gain its cooperation by using the promise of what it can expect from training. It becomes a quid pro quo arrangement where all elements of the self see the advantages of cooperating with one another.

As Guardian to the Gates of the Subconscious the mind is given the task of observing the main thoughts and themes it dwells upon, making sure our thoughts are in accordance with what 'we' want to manifest in our life. The subconscious does not censor the messages it receives from the mind, so it becomes the mind's function to be vigilant in monitoring what it thinks. This new responsibility gives the mind something different and unusual to do, and, desiring to be active, the mind accepts this task. We imprint the mythic titles into the mind time and time again, and eventually the mind accepts and understands the unique role it is to play in our evolving destiny.

The final title of the mind is Weaver of the Patterns. Each time the mind thinks thoughts, especially when they are charged with emotion, desire or intent, they become patterns of energy. As these thoughts are repeated again and again, they take on a very clear pattern and are picked up by the subconscious.

Many of the techniques of quantum mind power might seem, on the surface, to be deceptively simple, but they produce extraordinary results when we practice them regularly. However, the mind is lazy and set in its ways, so we have a real task in front us to gain back control. It is for this reason that we train daily. There are many different exercises we give the mind. The mind becomes bored easily and must be challenged and stimulated in a variety of different ways. We must keep the mind active in what we are doing, or it will fall back into its old habits. Being creative with our training and routines is our responsibility.

Working out in our mind is not unlike working out in the gym, where we train to become physically fit, building our stamina in the process. In the mental gym of our consciousness, we use mind power exercises to weave energy patterns and deepen our understanding. These practices strengthen and discipline the mind. By setting ourselves the task of doing the exercises, and following through with this, we also strengthen our will. The term willpower is not just a frivolous expression; there is real power in harnessing our will, and regular training will strengthen it. With a strong will we have the ability to execute and follow through on our best intentions.

Our warrior training begins with a series of mental exercises that we practice each day. Each day we set aside twenty or thirty minutes to work out in our mind. We can do more if we want to, and some will, but we don't have to do the exercises for hours to see results. Incredible results can be achieved in this short amount of time if we make it a daily habit. It is the daily part of the exercises that is the most important. It is far better to do twenty minutes every day than two hours once or twice a week; this is why I suggest limiting the session to twenty or thirty minutes. The goal is to make this training a daily habit.

CONTEMPLATION

The first exercise we practice is contemplation. I have chosen this exercise first because it is an excellent way to both exercise the mind and increase our understanding of the quantum maxims of the universe. We contemplate these laws, moving beyond surface understanding and intellectual curiosity to the deeper secrets they possess; in this way we can know, feel and understand them intimately.

Contemplation is directing the mind to 'think about' whatever statement, fact or law we have chosen for it. This practice has a dual benefit for us. The first and most obvious benefit is that when we contemplate something over a period of weeks and months we become more familiar with it. Depth of understanding and associate ideas build one upon another, and like puzzle pieces coming together, gradually a clearer, more intricate picture reveals itself to us. This is extremely valuable, for as we deepen our understanding of the laws of quantum reality something profound consolidates within us, and our ability to work with mind power is enhanced.

The second benefit, which I sometimes call the secret benefit, is that by focusing the mind in this particular way we are strengthening and disciplining the mind. The daily practice of contemplation gets the mind comfortable with taking directions and thinking the thoughts we choose for it, rather than the thoughts the mind has randomly chosen on its own, which is its natural tendency. Contemplation also plays to the mind's strength. The mind thinks thoughts and will do so whether we direct it or not, so letting it think thoughts but directing these thoughts in a specific way produces results for us while allowing the mind to do what it does naturally.

As we practice daily contemplations, very quickly a deeper understanding of what we are contemplating develops. We are amazed at how many new insights come to us, even in the first few days, but in truth these are but shadows of the depth of understanding that will be realized as we continue with this practice.

The objective of contemplation is to keep our mind focused on one concept, but within this concept letting the mind think about and associate with similar ideas. For example, if we are contemplating the quantum maxim, "Consciousness weaves and directs energy," we would set our mind the intention to think about this maxim. We begin by repeating the statement to ourselves, and then we notice what thoughts or ideas come up in our consciousness. As we contemplate, we might find ourselves thinking how receptive the web is, how responsive it is to our thoughts. If the web acts upon our thoughts, we realize, then we must be vigilant in what thoughts we entertain. Or we might find ourselves thinking what an extraordinary system this is, where consciousness interacts with the energy web. Contemplation reveals many ideas, thoughts, and concepts for us to ponder. We find ourselves coming up with insights we had not considered before.

During a five-minute period the mind will come up with many new and different thoughts about the theme we are contemplating. What will also happen is that the mind will become distracted and begin thinking about the evening's meal, or some errand that needs to be done tomorrow, and we suddenly find that we are not thinking about how consciousness directs energy at all, but have been totally distracted. As soon as we find our mind is not thinking about the statement we have given it we start again, directing the mind back to the original statement. It will surprise you how often the mind is distracted during a five-minute period, especially in the beginning stages of practicing this technique. Sometimes it is difficult to focus for even thirty seconds without getting distracted, but don't be discouraged by this. We don't measure our ability to concentrate by our first few attempts, which of course are going to be erratic. With practice our ability to focus and concentrate becomes much better.

The ancient Kabbalists practiced a variety of meditative methods, and descriptions of many of these practices have been preserved in manuscript form in both libraries and private collections. The sixteenth-century Kabbalist Judah Albotini shares light on one of their methods: "Those who meditate concentrate on an idea or on a very deep lesson. They close their eyes, and virtually nullify all their faculties in order to allow their hidden intellect to emerge from potential to action. They then absorb the lesson, permanently engraving it."[2]

Contemplating with this intensity, we become aware of insights and truths that were not apparent to us before we began practicing. By exercising in this way we are tapping directly into the hidden wisdom that is not really hidden at all, but exists beyond the mind's surface thoughts, awaiting our discovery.

Albotini also describes methods of "jumping" and "skipping."[3] This is using the process of what modern-day psychologists call "free association."[4] That is letting one thought or concept lead to another without censoring or trying to direct the process. According to Albotini, when one has attained great wisdom or a high state of awareness of a universal truth, the individual "engraves these revelations"[5] within himself. In quantum mind power we use the imprinting technique to do the very same thing. We engrave or 'imprint' the new insights we discover through contemplation directly into our subconscious, where they find fertile soil, where they becoming laws of power for us.

I must also speak briefly of the plateaus we reach as we embark upon regular contemplation practices, for if we do not understand the plateaus we will be tricked into discontinuing our practice after the first few attempts. When we first begin contemplating, often insights come so quickly and are so revealing that we are astounded. After just two or three times we are often amazed at what we have learned, but after a week of contemplating the same law or phrase we will have pierced through the surface levels of understanding. Here we quickly hit a plateau, where nothing new seems to be coming. It is as if we now know everything we need or can know about this particular area. We might have a week or two where nothing new is coming; it just seems to be the same old stuff over and over again. This is a plateau, and we might remain on this plateau for weeks before we can go deeper. Regular practice produces deeper insights, but this does not mean that every single day of contemplation brings us a slightly deeper understanding than the day before. Often there is a consolidation period, where nothing new seems to be happening, but really what is going on is that we are traversing an inner plateau, and this is a necessary process, part of the journey leading us to the next set of even deeper insights. Be persistent. Practice regularly. Trust the process.

The following quantum maxims, introduced in the previous chapter, are to be contemplated individually, deepening our understanding of them. This is also how we imprint them into our subconscious. We can take one a week and make each one the focus of our contemplation exercise. This way, in a one-year period we will have contemplated each one for thirteen weeks.

1. The consciousness that created the universe dwells within us.

2. We exist in the energy web and are one with it.

3. Consciousness weaves and directs energy.

4. Everything exists for us as a possibility.

By contemplating these quantum maxims daily, new insights are revealed to us. Choosing one quantum belief and focusing on it for five minutes is a valuable way to start each day. By contemplating these quantum maxims we are aligning ourselves with the laws of the universe, affirming our right and ability to work with these laws. Not only is it our right to weave and direct energy, it is the reason we were created. We are hardwired, designed and encouraged to work with the energy web, to create for ourselves whatever we choose. We are cosmic beings with a conscious mind, a subconscious mind, a body, and a soul, and through these different parts we have access to everything. We are encouraged by God/nature/evolution (choose your term) to create with these abilities according to our own unique vision. We let our mind 'think about' these truths. Contemplating these maxims changes who we are. Every maxim we contemplate will eventually become a belief within us, and as such become a law of power for us. In this way we re-create ourselves. What we focus on we become.

In training ourselves in these ways we become athletes of the mind. Our daily practices become our way of living, and we follow this path because we experience the benefits firsthand. We enjoy how we feel when we train. We see results in our life and this gives us the inspiration to continue. We have discovered a new way of living and we embrace this adventure.

SEVEN

Weaving the Web

"The word 'reality' does not have
the same meaning for all of us."
{ Eugene Wigner }

In the early 1990s, out-of-work actor Jim Carrey applied his thoughts, words and intentions in a very specific way to become the successful movie star he is today. As a struggling Canadian comic in Los Angeles, someone barely making ends meet, he set himself a very clear intention. He knew exactly what he wanted. He desired to be a famous and successful actor known throughout the world and earning fabulous amounts of money. To symbolize this intent he wrote himself a cheque for ten million dollars, and on the cheque he wrote "for acting services rendered." It was quite a stretch for him to imagine himself making ten million dollars for a single movie, since he was hardly working at all at the time, but he nonetheless wrote the cheque, put it in his wallet and took it out and looked at it every day. But he didn't just look at it. He imagined himself receiving this cheque over and over again, building a very clear pattern in his mind of this event happening. He would visualize it in his mind clearly, seeing it occur. He also used affirmations. "I've always believed in magic," Carrey reveals, "When I wasn't doing anything in this town, I'd go up every night, sit on Mulholland Drive, look out at the city, stretch out my arms and say, 'Everybody wants to work with me. I'm a really good actor. I have all kinds of movie offers.' I'd just repeat these things over and over." By doing this Carrey was weaving the web with his words. Words have a very specific energetic vibration. When we weave with our thoughts we call this visualization, and with our words, affirmations. He also harnessed his will and was determined to do whatever was necessary to achieve this goal, never wavering from this intent. Five years later, with his career soaring, he received ten million dollars for starring in the movie *Dumb and Dumber*.[1]

We weave the web with our thoughts, words, intentions and actions, and each of these methods has a particular technique associated with it. There are thousands of well-known athletes, artists and successful businessmen and women who have used these methods effectively to achieve success in their lives. Many of these stories I have already written about in my original book *Mind Power into the 21ˢᵗ Century*. While some of the following techniques might be familiar to those who have used mind power, I am including them in this chapter as they are a necessary foundation for the more advanced methods.

THE BASICS

Visualization is the technique of using our imagination to see and feel ourselves already possessing the goal we desire. It is a blueprint we create in our mind where we're imagining ourselves having or doing whatever it is we want to see happen in our life. We repeat these images over and over again, daily weaving the web. For a short, intense period of two to five minutes we focus our imagination, seeing ourselves closing the deal, having the relationship, healing the illness—whatever it is we wish to manifest. The key point to remember is that we always visualize ourselves already having the thing we want. This is the mental trick. We don't hope we'll achieve it, or have confidence that some day it will happen, we 'live and feel it' as if it is happening to us right now. The pattern of thought we weave is the image of our goal already having been achieved. During our exercise we think it has happened. This is the vibration we work with.

Our subconscious, which cannot distinguish between what is real and what is imagined, will act upon these images. We are 'weaving the web' with both our intent and these clear images. This technique is creating a pattern of energy that will attract from the quantum field of all possibilities the circumstances that most match these representations.

Now that we understand how consciousness and energy work together we can see the importance of creating clear mental images of what it is we wish to manifest.

With affirmations we use our words to achieve the same effect. Affirmations are statements we repeat to ourselves silently or out loud over and over again. This too is weaving the web, only this time it is with our words. We affirm whatever it is we want to see happen. For example, if we have an important interview coming up, we could affirm to ourselves, "A great interview," and we would repeat this statement over and over again for several minutes. Or let's say we're recovering from a leg injury; we could repeatedly say to ourselves, "My legs are strong and healthy."

Affirmations work because whatever we verbally repeat to ourselves will activate these thoughts. Say, "a great interview," and we will automatically begin thinking about our upcoming interview as "a great interview." Repeat, "I have strong and healthy legs," and our mind will begin imagining strong and healthy legs. Our words direct our thoughts. We repeat to ourselves exactly what we want to see happen without concerning ourselves with the details of how it will happen. We let our words vibrate our intentions and direct our thoughts. Carrey used the affirmations, "Everybody wants to work with me. I'm a really good actor. I have all kinds of movie offers."

Now note that when he was saying this to himself it was not true. Nobody wanted to work with him; he was broke and unemployed, and he could have just as easily repeated these words to himself, but he did not. He affirmed what he wanted to have happen to him. He was giving his subconscious very clear and accurate instructions. Affirmations vibrate our intentions. They weave the web in a very powerful way. This is probably the simplest and easiest of all the mind power techniques, and yet its effects can be quite dramatic. We should always have a variety of affirmations that we are working with daily. And we don't have to just say them; we can write them on a piece of paper, input them on our computer, text them to ourselves, or even sing them if we like.

I have a song called The Awakening Song that came to me during a vision quest almost ten years ago. It suddenly just began singing itself in me, and I was along for the ride. I sang it for about twenty minutes without stopping. It has countless verses, and strangely, it never sings itself the same way twice. I say that it sings itself because that's how it often feels. Sometimes I choose the verses but other times verses come out that I had not even thought about. The song sings what we need to hear. It always begins with the verse, "We are awakening in the vibrating matrix." The word matrix is Latin for womb. The 'vibrating matrix' is the womb of the energy web from which all things are birthed. This opening verse affirms our oneness with the matrix and reminds us that we are awakening. I will sing it for you if you go to www.learnmindpower.com. It is a very powerful song, a teaching song that resonates deeply with everyone who hears it. Many people now sing it. This song is a gift to us. We sing what is in our heart, and through this method we weave our reality. Sometimes we sing quantum truths over and over again, and by singing them they become melodic affirmation verses imprinting themselves into our subconscious. We sing our truths and what we desire to manifest and in this way we weave the web. This is a very creative way of using affirmations.

QUANTUM ALIGNMENT

We can align ourselves with whatever energy we choose simply by thinking about it. Consciousness allows us to do this. We must understand the basic fundamentals of physics and not be timid about working with energy in this way. Everything we wish to manifest, whether it is becoming financially successful, passing our college exams, healing an illness, becoming enlightened; each has a particular energetic vibration that creates this reality. Aligning with this vibration in consciousness puts us in contact with it. The energy web contains the energy signature of everything we want or need. It is receptive and ever ready to act upon our instructions.

Using the technique of quantum alignment, we vibrate the energetic qualities of success, health, abundance, courage, or whatever we wish to create for ourselves. We connect to the source vibration of these realities. This is not hard to do. Using our imagination we feel ourselves connecting with the fundamental energy that creates all things. We connect directly to the energy web. Using our imagination in this way is not 'make-believe'; it is a real way of weaving energy. We can do this because we are one with everything, and because consciousness directs energy. Our quantum capabilities allow us to do this. By harnessing both our will and imagination we can contact anything in the energy web system.

If we are sick, for example, through quantum alignment we can access health energy by focusing on the energetic vibration that creates and maintains abundant health—not just in us but in all things. This is the key point. We aren't accessing our own personal energy and trying to increase it; rather we are connecting and aligning with archetypical health energy that resonates as a vibrational signature in the quantum field. Abundant health, whether it is the health of a tree, a whale or a strong athlete has a particular resonance. We are now working in the dimension of quantum reality. We align ourselves with this web vibration simply by thinking about it. With our imagination (which has been strengthened through exercises), we let this vibration fill our consciousness and flood through our body. If we choose to, we can direct this energy to whatever area of our body requires healing, but this is unnecessary, for simply vibrating the energy will cause it to quite naturally find the areas that need attention. In fact, it knows better than we where this energy needs to be assimilated.

We may think of the health of a strong lion as it stalks its prey, the strength of a giant cedar tree, the virility of a champion athlete at the peak of his or her ability, and use these examples as energy sources with which we can align. The health, vitality and strength contained within them become ours while we are aligning with them in consciousness.

If we were working with the Newtonian model where everything is separate and independent—which is the way our reality appears to our senses—what I'm suggesting would be impossible. In fact doing this technique would be ridiculously naïve and unproductive, but fortunately this is not the world we live in. We live in a quantum world where our reality not only allows us to do such things but actually encourages us to interact in these ways. As quantum warriors we have the ability to access the web in these new, revolutionary ways.

If we wish to attract financial success, using this method we would connect with the energy web, acknowledging our oneness with it. Then we 'tune-in' to the vibrational resonance of financial abundance.

We would vibrate with the energy of abundance. We could think of extremely successful companies with all the talented, highly paid people working for them and connect with this energy, aligning with it in our imagination. We could think of a philanthropist giving away millions of dollars, or of any successful entrepreneur, artist or athlete who makes lots of money, and connect with the energy of their financial success. Now let me be very clear, we're not trying to pretend we are these people or that we inhabit their lives; rather we are connecting with the vibrational frequency that creates financial abundance. It is the archetypical energy pattern vibrating throughout the energy web we are connecting with. With practice we will be able to align with any energetic vibration we wish. By doing this we attract to ourselves the people, circumstances and events that are in alignment with this energy. As I shared with you in the opening chapter, it is through this method that I first aligned myself with the abundance vibration by resonating this vibration every opportunity I could, attracting the circumstances that led to my success.

We must understand our relationship with the energy web. This connection must be well established. Actually we are always connected to the energy web and one with it, but our mind does not know this and thinks we are separate, so work is required. We practice aligning with the web, feeling its power and immensity, affirming our oneness with it. As we align regularly with the web in this way our connection is realized and we come to know our oneness. We now have the means to work with energy and consciousness in ways we did not possess before.

Having this ability comes with practice. This is where our training comes to our assistance. We contemplate the energy web being responsive to us. We let our mind "think about" the quantum maxims, feeling our connection with the universe, and we do this hundreds of times. Yes, hundreds, even thousands of times. Quantum mind power is a practice, and over a period of months and years—one never stops these exercises—we build our relationship with the web, and we find it is easy to weave thought patterns and connect with archetypical energy in the ways I'm suggesting. If we had not put in the training and done these preliminary exercises it would be difficult to imagine that this would be possible, but because we have trained ourselves, quantum alignment becomes something quite natural. This is yoga of the mind. Through daily exercises we expand our capacities of working with the web. What seems difficult at first eventually becomes effortless when we practice it many times. It is much like when we first learned to ride a bicycle. At first it seemed impossible, but once we got it, it was easy, and we have never lost the ability. The same applies to quantum alignment. The biggest hurdle is our doubt that we can do it. With practice we will find this is easier than we originally thought, and the results we obtain will speak for themselves. This is what is so exciting about these times; we are on the frontier of working with energy and consciousness in new and innovative ways.

ACTION

Earlier in this chapter I shared the story of Jim Carrey writing himself a cheque for ten million dollars, and then five years later earning that amount. If only it was that simple. What was not fully explained, what was left unsaid, is how much work and creativity also contributed to his success. It didn't just happen overnight, and there was more involved than him thinking thoughts and willing it to happen. Carrey diligently honed his skills as a comedian in hundreds of small clubs around North America, trying out skits, perfecting his comic timing and instincts. He mastered the visual medium first as a regular on the TV program *In Living Color*, and then as a film actor. It was this creative action—combined with his mind power—that created the opportunity to realize his dream. It happened because Carrey knew that to be successful you must do more than just think about success; you must act in meaningful ways, attracting the circumstances that make it happen. If we want a healthy body, a promotion, a million dollars, enlightenment or any other goal we have envisioned for ourselves, we need to do more than just weave the web with our thoughts and then sit back hoping for the best. Our mind power must be combined with daily action. For example, if we wanted a meaningful relationship we would practice mind power techniques, seeing and feeling ourselves already in this relationship. And we would act in a way that attracts the possibility of meeting someone, whether this is joining new clubs, going to social events, approaching people we find attractive, etc. So too in winning a sporting event. We would think about winning the event using mind power techniques. And we would also act in ways that attract the possibility of winning, including training regularly, eating well, competing against the best competition we can find, and so on.

I'm amazed at how some people think that simply by using mind power and mind power alone they will achieve their goals. Occasionally I will have students or readers of my books come up to me and say something like, "John, I've been doing my exercises every day now for sixty days and nothing is happening." I usually ask them, "What else have you been doing?" Quite often my question is met with stunned silence, as if the mind power exercises by themselves should be enough. Let me be very clear. If we want to lose twenty pounds but refuse to eat well, exercise, and change the habits that created the extra weight in the first place, affirmations by themselves probably won't work. If we want to become financially successful but don't set goals, have plans and act upon them in meaningful ways, we can visualize all we want and we're probably going to remain where we are. Maybe in some other altered reality we have yet to experience we only need to hope and think about something and it will happen automatically, but here in this world action is required.

Goals are the focus that directs our actions and the means by which we can achieve our success. Goals are not vague hopes or desires; they are clearly defined objectives that are measurable and have a time frame associated with them. Without goals and deadlines almost nothing is achieved, because procrastination and inertia take hold.

To achieve a goal we start with the end in mind, having a clear image of what we want to achieve, organizing and executing activities around the priorities we establish. We take it one day at a time. We focus on what we can do today. Each day we take the steps which move us closer to our goal. We know more will be revealed to us tomorrow and still more the day after. Day by day, week by week, month by month we call upon ourselves to be our best. We have a clear vision of what we wish to achieve and daily we work towards it, letting nothing stand in our way. We have the will of a warrior and we weave the web with our thoughts and actions. Acting daily in concrete ways towards our vision sets in motion alchemy that works in powerful and mysterious ways.

INVOKING SYNCHRONICITY

When we dare to believe in quantum possibilities and act daily in meaningful ways using our thoughts and actions, the powers of the universe come to assist us. We are greeted with fortuitous events and meaningful coincidences regularly. We attract from the quantum source of all possibilities the exact people and circumstances that are required at every point of our journey. This is not magic or luck; it is simply how the system works. Just as the spider is sensitive to the least movement in its web, so the energy web is sensitive to the vibrations of everything that happens within it. Every vibrational change is immediately registered; nothing goes unnoticed. We are one with everything, and so we invoke synchronicity into our lives by understanding and aligning in consciousness with this connection.

Carl Jung[2] defined synchronicity as "a meaningful coincidence of two or more events, where something other than probability of chance is involved." Synchronicity to Jung meant the strange and unusual encounters or events which happen to individuals that appear on the surface to have no causal effect, and yet have such a profound meaning to the individual that it was unlikely to be the result of mere chance. They happen to all of us, and usually we explain them away as being a lucky coincidence, which in fact they might be, but there is also the possibility that something deeper and more meaningful is at work at these times.

A colleague of Jung shared the fact that the more Jung relied on his unconscious and trusted it the more it worked for him. "I observed one concrete fact, for instance, in watching Dr. Jung—the older he became the more he got the information he needed for whatever he was thinking about or working on; it simply ran after him."[3]

Once when Jung was occupied with a specific problem, a general practitioner in Australia sent him a complete package of the material he needed, and it arrived by mail just at the very instant Jung said, "Now I ought to have some observations on that kind of thing." He voiced the words and there was a knock at the door. This is something you notice.

Jung referred to these types of circumstances as "magic causality." He strongly suspected that such causality has its source in the unconscious, yet he struggled to find a way to have it accepted by the scientific community. Nor did he understand fully how it worked. While Jung was familiar with the most up-to-date scientific discoveries of his day, and had contact with Niels Bohr and Albert Einstein, the most explosive findings of quantum physics had yet to be revealed. We in the twenty-first century can more easily understand why synchronicity works, even if it still seems incredible to us. It is simply the energy web in action.

A close friend shared a dramatic example of a synchronistic event that happened to her when she was a young girl. She was at that time a thirteen-year-old girl who was, as she termed it, "on fire for God." She would travel on the bus every Saturday "looking to do God's work." She believed that God was calling her to do his work in the world, and so every Saturday she set off looking for opportunities. She rode the bus to wherever felt appropriate, and often extraordinary things happened, but nothing could prepare her for what would happen this particular Saturday. She was riding the bus when suddenly she felt an overpowering urge to get off the bus immediately. Across from the bus stop was a hotel, and she was led into the hotel bar without knowing why. Now it is illegal in Canada for anyone under the age of nineteen to be in a bar, and being a young-looking thirteen, she was obviously not of age, and yet no one stopped her or said a word to her, even though one waiter looked right at her. "It was as if I was invisible," she said recounting the incident. For some unknown reason she walked directly to a women who was sitting alone at a table and sat down. "God has asked me to tell you he loves you and you are not alone," she said, as if the words were coming from someone else. She had no idea why she had just said these words, or what the woman's reaction would be. The woman just sat, looked at her in disbelief for several seconds, and then she burst into tears.

"Yesterday I bought a gun," she said, going on to describe the horrific circumstances she was living under, how hopeless and alone she felt. "This afternoon at one o'clock I said to myself, 'If God does not send me a sign or give me some hope in the next hour, I am going to kill myself.'" They both looked at the clock—it was ten minutes to two. In ten more minutes she planned to climb the shabby hotel stairs to her room and kill herself. The two wept in each other's arms, and then my friend left, never to see the woman again.

How could this strange occurrence have happened? Obviously something more than luck or coincidence was at work. The quantum theory of interconnectedness explains it. Each of us is part of the same vibrating matrix, and there is no reason to doubt that, in extraordinary circumstances, we are led to events that serve purposes beyond our understanding. Somehow the depth of that woman's despair and the intent of the young girl to do good were matched, and the two were drawn together. The universe works like this, in more ways than we suspect.

Psychologist and author Jean Houston shares having a conversation with the illustrious anthropologist Margaret Mead. She had noticed that Mead experienced an extraordinary number of fortuitous events. She always seemed to be in the right place at the right time. Jean commented on this to Mead one day. "You are so blessed," she said.

"Yes, I know," Mead replied.

"Why?" Houston questioned further.

Margaret Mead looked at her for a moment, and then in a gruff voice answered, "Because I expect to be."[4]

Could it be that simple?

Novelist Somerset Maugham said it another way: "It's a funny thing about life; if you refuse to accept anything but the best, you very often get it."[5]

Meeting my listening mentor, Annie, was a synchronistic event that changed the trajectory of my life, and I will share this story in a later chapter. I have experienced many synchronistic events, most of us have, and the more we believe in them the more they occur. We invoke synchronicity by believing in an open, dynamic universe where all is possible, where our thoughts and desires are heard and acted upon. As scholar and author Joseph Campbell said, " . . . a thousand unseen helping hands"[6] come to our aid when we embark on a course of action that has passion for us. Is this possible? Goethe certainly thought so. He wrote, "Man of ability and action, be worthy of, and expect grace from those that are great, favour from the powerful, a helping hand from those who are active and good, affection from the crowd, love from an individual."[7] His meteoric career in the eighteenth-century German court supported his belief.

As we accept our oneness with all things, we invoke synchronicity in our lives just by being who we are. Our thoughts, beliefs and actions resonate in the energy web, attracting to us the most amazing circumstances. The minute we are willing to accept help from this "invisible collaborator," we will attract it everywhere in our life. From both the seen and unseen, from that which we understand and that which is still mysterious, remarkable things will happen for us.

EIGHT

The Subconscious

"The subconscious is the part of us
that is connected to all that is."
{ Sylvia Bak[1] }

Evolution has equipped us with two minds, not just one. One mind, it seems, is not enough for what our destiny has in store for us. These two minds are vastly different from one another, but they are designed to complement one another, working together as a functioning team. This, however, rarely happens, and this breakdown is one of the reasons we have problems in our lives. We seldom give our subconscious any thought, much less work with it in creative ways. As a good friend of mine once said, "My relationship with my subconscious is more or less like my relationship with my liver. I'm aware of its existence, but that's about it."

We must reclaim our subconscious and have it working for us in the ways it was designed. Our subconscious mind is an extraordinary part of who we are and will help us immensely when we work closely with it. The advantages of having our conscious and subconscious minds working together become obvious as we deepen our understanding of who we are. Our subconscious is the means by which we manifest our reality. Suddenly it seems ridiculous that we have been ignoring this part of ourselves.

The first mythic title of the subconscious is Holder of the Patterns. Our conscious mind, you will remember, is Weaver of the Patterns. The similarity between these two titles indicates clearly how the conscious and subconscious minds work together. Our conscious mind weaves patterns of thought and our subconscious receives and holds these patterns as vibrational imprints. It is through daily repetition that the conscious mind imprints patterns into the subconscious. This again underscores the importance of our daily exercises.

The second title of the subconscious is Communicator with the Web. The thought patterns held in our subconscious vibrate their messages day and night. They 'communicate' with the web by sending out vibrational signals. Vibrations are the language of the universe, and the subconscious and the energy web are in constant communication with each other through this medium.

As I mentioned earlier, in the Kabbalistic teachings each human being is considered to be a microcosm of the macrocosm, a little universe in miniature. Kabbalah equates the subconscious and the energy web as the same function, and it calls this sphere of activity *Yesod*. When functioning in us *Yesod* is the subconscious, and when functioning in the universe it is the energy web.

Contemplating how *Yesod* works brings about what Kabbalists call the "Vision of the Machinery of the Universe." And when we understand the unique relationship that exists between our subconscious and the energy web, we do indeed have a vision of how the universe works. This extraordinary insight into the nature of reality reveals to us how we can use this relationship to create whatever we desire. The method is crystal clear: whatever circumstances we wish to manifest, we simply create very clear thought patterns of these situations in our mind. Daily repetition of these images transfers these patterns to the subconscious. This happens automatically, without us having to direct it or even think about it. Once these patterns are received and anchored within our subconscious, it communicates these images throughout the energy web.

In many ways the subconscious and the energy web are very similar to one another. The subconscious functions in us in exactly the same way the energy web functions in the universe. The subconscious and the energy web are both designed to be receptive to inputs from beyond themselves. The subconscious accepts patterns from the conscious mind, and the energy web accepts patterns from the subconscious. Once the energy web receives instructions from our subconscious it vibrates these 'energetic' signals throughout the entire system, where these signals are noticed by the trillions of connections contained within the web. Not all will respond; only those connections which feel vibrationally 'called to act' (through a means none of us fully understand) will respond, setting in motion a process by which circumstances, people and opportunities come into our life.

Whatever we wish to create in our life, our first and most important step is to give our subconscious a very clear pattern to work with. Daily we contemplate the relationship that exists between our subconscious and the energy web, and as we build our understanding we see clearly how our reality unfolds. As we deepen our understanding of our subconscious we deepen our understanding of the energy web, and vice versa. Contemplating one gives us insight into the other, and by cross-referencing our different insights we gain valuable understanding of "the machinery of the universe."

One very curious aspect of our subconscious is that it cannot tell the difference between what is real and what is imagined. This at first might seem like an extraordinary deficiency on the part of our subconscious, but actually it is not. Our subconscious is specifically designed this way so that it can receive patterns and work with them without question. The implications of this are far reaching. For example, when we do a mind power exercise such as visualization, our conscious mind is aware that this visualization is a creation of the mind and not 'real' in any absolute sense, but the subconscious does not make this distinction. It accepts these images unquestioningly, and when these images are repeated time and time again they become wired within.

There have not been a lot of scientific experiments exploring the potentials of the subconscious; studying this mysterious part of ourselves has mostly been left to psychologists and mystics. There was, however, an experiment involving amputees with 'phantom limb syndrome' that illustrates the potential of what we can do with our subconscious mind.

Amputees often report pain in their phantom limbs because of their inability to move or interact with that limb. While some might dismiss this as "only in their mind," it is a real problem for those who experience it. Researchers, trying to devise a way to help subjects with this pain, designed a special apparatus whereby they could 'trick' the subconscious. They constructed a boxlike structure where both arms could be inserted into openings; one side of the box was exposed, on the other side they placed a mirror in front of the opening. Amputees put their good arm in the side of the box where they could see it and the amputated arm into the opening behind the mirror. When the patient flexed his good arm he would see it flexing, and when he looked at the amputated arm, which was hidden behind the mirror, he would see the mirror image of his other arm flexing, giving the appearance of the phantom arm flexing. Now the conscious mind of course knew this was all a set-up, that the phantom arm was not actually moving, in fact did not exist, but the subconscious mind accepted the mirror image, accepted that the arm was in fact moving. Incredibly, within weeks of regular practice most patients reported the pain in their phantom arm had diminished or disappeared.[2] Procedures using similar techniques with stroke victims and other physical rehabilitation patients cannot be far behind.

Another striking difference between our two minds is that while the conscious mind is the Custodian of the Will, the subconscious mind has no will or volition of its own. It is passive in reaction to what it receives, acting mechanically, according to the patterns it already holds. In fact, you could say that all of mind power is based upon the receptivity of the subconscious to suggestion and instruction. The subconscious does not choose which patterns it will vibrate, nor does it judge or censor what it receives from the conscious mind. Like neurons that wire together because of constant traffic, the subconscious accepts content delivered to it through repetition. Whatever themes the conscious mind regularly dwells upon, whether positive or negative, will become a vibrational pattern, which our subconscious will then communicate to the web. This vibration becomes our personal energy signature, and by this vibration we are known. Our most intimate hopes, fears and desires are not secrets whispered only to ourselves; they are resonating vibrations spread throughout the entire energy web. The energy web knows us intimately. There are no secrets in the universe.

SUCCESS VIBRATION

The third mythic title of the subconscious is "The Engine of Success." Some might argue that we could also call our subconscious the engine of our failure, and this too is true, for it will accurately vibrate whatever patterns we hold within. However, we choose to call it the engine of success, and by giving it this title we are clearly vibrating this intention. We also keep this engine well lubricated with success thoughts. Daily we weave patterns of thought that accurately reflect the vision of what we intend to manifest. Our subconscious is our partner in success, and it is up to us to support this partner in every way we can. Our conscious mind weaves the patterns and the subconscious communicates these to the web. This is how the system works.

It is our warrior duty to be successful at the tasks we set for ourselves, both large and small. Whether it is helping our children with their homework, cooking a nutritious meal, closing a business deal, training the mind or becoming awakened, we are called to be our best in every situation, to be successful. Actually we are already very successful in many areas of our life; it's just that we've forgotten to acknowledge ourselves for this. We should acknowledge and appreciate our ability to be successful in the little things as well as the big, and in this way we build within ourselves a success vibration.

When we think of ourselves as successful we are fuelling our engine with success vibrations. When we think of ourselves as failures, weak and unworthy, we are sending our subconscious the wrong messages. Our subconscious needs us to cooperate with it in a proactive way. It cannot be our engine of success if we do not provide it with successful thoughts. As quantum warriors we are responsible for not just what we do, but what we think as well. We are responsible for weaving thoughts of success so that the subconscious can have these patterns to work with. We understand clearly both the relationship between the conscious and subconscious mind, and the relationship between the subconscious mind and the energy web. It is our understanding of these relationships that gives us clarity and direction in our daily exercises.

Each of us has been programmed with a strong inner urge for success, and while our concepts of success may differ wildly, the desire for achieving success is exactly the same for all of us. It is an inherent part of who we are. The fact that each of us possesses this compelling desire should give us a clue to the meaning and purpose of our lives. The universe has designed and wired us to be successful. It is through each of our successes that the universe creatively expresses itself. Unfortunately, our culture's preoccupation with the consumption of things has confused us. We've mistaken having lots of possessions for being successful. Having more and more things in our life will never make us successful, even if these things are fancy cars, yachts and mansions. As warriors we define our success in a more expansive way that reflects the larger vision of what it means to be a human being. We need to move beyond just stuff and think of character, values, integrity, and how we can be of help to others, and include these nonmaterial aspects in our vision of what it means to be successful. We should think seriously about our core values, what is important to us, what we truly want to be in this life. Until we have done this we will confuse ourselves by wanting everything, and in this we will never be satisfied, for there will always be something more we need, no matter how much we already possess.

LIGHT SHADOW–DARK SHADOW: EXPLORING THE UNCONSCIOUS

It was Jung who first used the word shadow to describe the mysterious unconscious. We are fortunate to have the teachings and discoveries of those who have preceded us. On the shoulders of our ancestors we stand and are able to explore places we could never have reached on our own. In warrior mythology we have taken the concept of shadow and further expanded it into light and dark shadow. While some traditional Jungian psychologists might object to this liberty, it has its advantages. It allows us to look at both aspects of our shadow and approach them in different ways. Ultimately, any model will be judged by its effectiveness in day-to-day living, and our warrior model will stand this test.

The shadow is everything within us that is unconscious, undeveloped or denied. It is what poet Robert Bly called "the long black bag" we carry around with us. The bag is black because its contents are unseen by the conscious mind, and it is long because it contains everything we are.[3]

Our shadow patterns are dynamic factors independent of our

conscious intentions. They often surprise and overwhelm us with emotions, moods, dreams, fears and desires, acting in ways that are purposeful. That is, the subconscious, while possessing no will, has a very definite mandate to which it is committed. It must and will vibrate the patterns it holds, weaving the web with whatever is contained within it. Shadow work is getting to know and understand the dynamic functions that are operating within us on a subconscious level. We call this process 'personal archaeology,' and it is the detective work of examining our life to identify underlying patterns that often do not on the surface make sense to us. In fact, most of our patterns are completely unknown to us. This is something we must take into account, for many are the mysteries that exist in our uncharted shadow world.

THE LIGHT SHADOW

Our light shadow contains our unclaimed positive potentials, the parts of us that we have not yet brought to fruition. They are the gifts, talents and unexplored abilities we possess that lie hidden and unused. Because we are a holographic piece of the overall design of the universe, everything that is possible and good and excellent is potentially part of our light shadow, and while theoretically true, practically speaking, some things are more available to us than others. Not all talents and gifts within the universe are ours to use, at least not in this particular lifetime. Some are more difficult to access, while others are just below the surface, waiting like seeds in a dried-out riverbed for the rains of our attention to supply them with the energy needed to reveal themselves.

Our light shadow is discovered by following our bliss, our natural talents, our joys and our creativity, and letting these parts of us lead us to where they want to go. Trusting what is fun and joyful leads us to our light shadow. Whatever is intriguing has meaning for us. Shadow work is not logical. It is intuitive. In this work we go where we 'feel' we should, not where we 'think' we should. In shadow work our feelings always lead and our logic follows. Embarking on this path invigorates us like nothing else can.

The forces of evolution want us to access our light shadow. We are encouraged by the universe to uplift ourselves and become talented, enlightened and wondrous. In discovering our hidden potentials we not only nourish ourselves by uplifting ourselves, we uplift and nourish the whole. These talents, once awakened, weave the web with our new abilities, bringing blessings, insights and gifts to many. Our cosmic consciousness, latent within us, calls for us to increase who we are and bring to fruition our hidden abilities.

There is biblical scripture which illustrates this point: "For the kingdom of heaven is as a man travelling into a far country, who called his own servants, and delivered unto them his goods. And to one he gave five talents, to another two, and to another one . . ." The parable goes on to describe how the servant who was given five talents (coins used in biblical times) traded and turned the five talents into ten. The one who had two did the same and ended up with four, but the one who had only one talent was fearful of losing his coin, so he buried his talent and did nothing with it. When the master later returned from his travels and asked for an accounting, he was very pleased with the two who had used their talents to increase their holdings. In fact they were rewarded for doing so, "Well done, thou good and faithful servants; thou hast been faithful over a few things. I will make thee ruler over many things." But toward the servant who did nothing the master was very displeased, and he cast him out.[4]

The message is clear. We are required to increase who we are. The energy web rewards us when we awaken our light shadow, letting it bear fruit and shine onto the world. When we take the initiative to access our light shadow we are rewarded every step of the way, for integrating our light shadow into our lives is the path of making us whole.

THE DARK SHADOW

The Dark Shadow contains the parts of us that are often disruptive, in that they usually hold us back or cause us problems. Anything that is unconscious and exists within us, literally sharing our lives with us, must be examined and understood. This is why shadow work is so valuable. It is our subconscious beliefs that often keep us stuck in the various problem areas of our life.

The dark shadow contains hidden patterns which often absorb vast amounts of energy, leaving us feeling depleted, anxious, frustrated, and at the mercy of forces we do not understand. Often we act in ways that seem irrational and counterproductive. Since they are unconscious, we do not see our dark-shadow beliefs, but we certainly see and experience their effects in our life.

Jung said, "Everyone carries a shadow . . . it forms an unconscious snag, thwarting our most well-meant intentions."[5] A Jungian psychologist, adding to this, once said to me, "If we do not own our shadow, our shadow owns us."

Patterns are the hidden footprints of the subconscious. Most of us have patterns in our life that defy logic, and no matter how many times we try to change these patterns, they seem to have a power of their own that overrides our best intentions. We achieve success in some areas of our lives, and yet in other areas, no matter what we do, success doesn't seem to materialize. Why is this? In most cases the reason is simply that we have subconscious beliefs that undermine our best intentions and desires. Here is an important fact of our quantum reality that we must understand: when our desires are in conflict with subconscious beliefs the subconscious beliefs will always dominate. This is why even our most important goals often do not manifest—what we desire is being countered by what we believe on a subconscious level.

Energywise, our belief patterns have more power than our desires. This is why in an earlier chapter I emphasized the importance of establishing foundation beliefs. Our subconscious beliefs are constantly having an effect in our life, whether we are aware of them or not. While we often do not know or understand the beliefs we hold subconsciously, we can usually recognize dysfunctional patterns in our life and through this deduce what might be in shadow. Unconscious patterns tend to be quite routine, which allows us to detect them through personal archaeology.

Let me share with you a past pattern of mine that for over twenty years was part of my dark shadow. Throughout my early adult life I had the pattern of leaving relationships. It was very strange because I wouldn't leave when the relationship was going badly, but rather when it was going well. This happened time and time again in my life. Then one day in my midforties, while I was practicing a holotropic breathing exercise, my subconscious revealed something startling to me. What popped into my mind, out of nowhere (my subconscious), was the thought, "My mother didn't leave me because 'I wasn't good enough.' "

"What a strange thought," I observed to myself, "She didn't leave me at all."

Now a little background information: when I was thirteen my mother drowned. It was traumatic, as you can imagine, but I dealt with it as best I could, and it appeared to have no lasting effect. I grew up to be a confident, successful, well-balanced person enjoying my life, yet with an unusual pattern in my relationships. Now here I was, in my forties, and all at once I got it: My subconscious mind had misinterpreted the drowning of my mother as her leaving me, which symbolically was correct, and deduced (incorrectly) that the reason she left me was because I wasn't good enough. Here is where it gets very interesting; my subconscious, wishing to protect me, decided that it was dangerous to love a woman, so to protect me from ever being hurt by a woman again it had me leave relationships when they became too intimate. Notice I say my subconscious made this decision, because none of this was conscious for me until that very moment. Suddenly the reason for my leaving relationships became crystal clear. Once I understood what my subconscious had created within me, it was no longer in shadow. The belief pattern still existed, but now I knew it was there and I had the ability to work with it.

Most of us will recall a Grimm Brothers fairy tale titled *Rumpelstiltskin*. In this story the heroine is held under threat of giving up her first-born child by a devious character called Rumpelstiltskin, and she will not be freed from her obligation to him until she can tell him his name, which is unknown to her. She tries repeatedly, without success, to discover his name, but finally it is revealed to her by a messenger. Once she utters Rumpelstiltskin's name to him, his power over her is destroyed and she is free to live her life as she pleases.

Often fairy tales contain within them psychological truths, and this tale certainly represents the power a dark shadow has over us, but like the heroine in the tale, once we can identify our dark shadow by name, we release ourselves from its power.

Now that I knew my dark-shadow belief, it no longer had unconscious control over me. It still had power and needed to be changed, but that was the easy part. I immediately began reprogramming a new set of beliefs about relationships and the woman I intended to attract. There was no doubt in my mind that I would now attract someone very special. My connection to the web, at this point of my life, was well established and my desire was clear. The only question remaining was who would she be?

I began programming for a woman who would possess what I felt were the three most important qualities I wanted in my future partner, what I called the three S's. I began projecting for a woman who was smart, sexy and spiritual. Almost six months later I met the most amazing woman who was smart, sexy and spiritual, but she had even more than the three S's I had been projecting. She had two extra S's, for a total of five. She was smart, sexy, spiritual, sophisticated (a bonus), and the last S really made me laugh. Her name was Sylvia. Understanding how the subconscious works, you can imagine my amusement over the fact that her name would also begin with S. But that is how the subconscious works. It focused on the S part because, in hindsight, that is what I focused on, and it gave me two extra. Of course I didn't have to leave this time, because the old shadow belief (that relationships were unsafe and dangerous) had been replaced with new ones, and now, close to twenty years later, we are happily married and I am more in love with my wife today than I was the day I married her. Had this belief pattern not been detected and corrected this could never have happened.

Recently I was interviewing a woman who wanted to participate in my five-day Awakening program. During our interview she told me a story that again emphasizes the importance of giving the subconscious very clear instructions, with no ambiguity. She was a mechanical engineer and had wanted to manifest lots of money, so she gave her subconscious the affirmation, "I'm going to make lots and lots of money." And she used this as a daily mantra, repeating it many times over a four-month period.

After those four months, it didn't seem to be working; in fact she lost her job before finding a new one. But it was the nature of her new job that reflected the affirmation perfectly, although not in the way she had planned. She now works for the government, overseeing the printing of the nation's currency. She literally 'makes' lots of money.

"It's not what I had expected," she said laughing, but it once again demonstrates how the subconscious works.

These examples highlight once again why the mythic title of the conscious mind is Guardian to the Gates of the Subconscious. Now that we understand the enormous power a belief pattern resonating in our subconscious possesses, we see the importance of being vigilant in allowing only the best and most empowering beliefs to reside in this engine of manifestation.

SHADOW CRISIS AND THE SHADOW GAME

I was lucky that my shadow pattern of leaving relationships was revealed to me in such an obvious way. It doesn't always happen so easily. But it does happen when we examine our life, observe our patterns, and are willing to do the necessary inner work. Shadow work always brings benefits, and our shadow parts are always trying to make contact. We, however, are often reluctant to do the work, face ourselves, and make the necessary changes. Often we only deal with our shadow when a misfortune or tragedy forces us to look for answers we can't provide. This is why personal crises are so often valuable—both light and dark shadows often emerge and reveal themselves during the turmoil. It happens this way if we are willing to face ourselves honestly, but this is typically not our first reaction when crisis occurs. Usually we are looking for a quick fix, so that we can go right back to the way things used to be. But, in the wake of a life crisis, things are not meant to go back to where they were before. The whole purpose of the emergence of a shadow crisis is that it is calling for a change. Something new must be birthed, or something old sacrificed. All shadow work is either birth or death. When crisis comes we must ask ourselves, what needs to be changed? How can I shift the energy of this situation? Real life-changes are required in shadow work. This is how we play the shadow game; we always ask ourselves what needs to be birthed (brought to fruition) or killed (changed or eliminated). There is always a sacrifice involved.

Sacrifice is something that is often misunderstood. It sounds unpleasant but really it is just an exchange of energy. For example, we sacrifice fifteen dollars so we can go to a movie. We sacrifice watching TV or playing video games so we can work out at the gym and get physically fit. Sacrifice allows energy to be redirected into something else. We must not be ignorant about what is required to travel the shadow path. We have to be willing to take the sword to that which no longer serves us.

Often inappropriate desires and habits are sacrificed, and this works to our benefit. Sometimes we sacrifice our laziness or our self-pity, or maybe even our ambition in order to move ahead. We sacrifice old beliefs, dysfunctional habits, aspects of ourselves that do not serve us. New ways of living take the place of the old and our priorities change. The shadow game is like a dance where we move about all over the floor, back and forth, round and round. It is not a straight line to a clear destination. It is not logical and it can drive the mind crazy, but other parts of us come to our aid. We feel and intuit and spend time not knowing before we eventually get a sense of what is happening, but we are always rewarded for this effort. The emergence of both light and dark shadow is always a positive event in our lives; it is to be welcomed. It is a way of getting to know ourselves. It moves us in the directions we are meant to go, and we flow with the movement, trusting this unknown current.

THE COLLECTIVE UNCONSCIOUS

Now we explore even deeper the mystery of ourselves. It is not just our own subconscious we must be aware of. We must also know that within us ebbs and flows the tides of the collective unconscious. The collective unconscious is the great sea of information that contains the collected patterns of everything that has ever occurred in time and space. It contains archetypical forces and original patterns emanating from the beginning of time onwards.

In the Carlos Castaneda books, the sorcerer Don Juan has an excellent way of explaining this principle to his apprentice Carlos. He instructs Carlos to put various objects on a table, which has been set outside, and tells him that each of the objects represents Carlos's various preferences, habits and normal ways of thinking. What's on the tabletop represents his conscious mind. Don Juan then tells Carlos to look under the table to see what is there. What is under the table represents his subconscious, and Don Juan advises Carlos that he must know and understand the contents of what resides here as well.

Prompted by Don Juan, Carlos walks a considerable distance up a hill, turns and looks down at the small table, now quite far off. Carlos is told to look away from the table, in all directions, at the vastness of this reality compared to the small table, and what is under the table. This, he is told, is the collective unconscious.

The point he is impressing upon Carlos is the immensity of the collective unconscious, and using this analogy, Carlos begins to understand that the collective unconscious exists everywhere, that he is part of something infinitely greater than he had supposed. Now it is not just the table and what is under the table that he must account for, but rather the entire universe too.[6]

It is in the collective unconscious that the archetypical patterns of the human experience reside. To imagine that we are uninfluenced by the tides and movements of the collective is to live an illusion. The collective is always at work, influencing us in many ways, and we must always account for this in the greater scheme of things.

It is commonly believed that archetypical patterns such as greed, hate, shame, compassion, wisdom, self-pity and arrogance, to name but a few, have been woven into the collective unconscious by the repeated thought patterns of humans thinking and vibrating these patterns for as long as our species has been around, and this is possible. Another possibility, as incredible as it is going to sound, is that these archetypical patterns have always existed, and they have been designed to be part of the game. They have been inserted into the web from the beginning of time, for the specific purpose of both thwarting and uplifting us, each in their own particular way. If this dimension of time and space is just one of the games in a metaverse that has perhaps billions of different games, it is not inconceivable that the universe would want to 'test' the abilities of our species, to see how well we can navigate through these aspects before we are able to move on. Looking at it this way, the archetypes become much more interesting, and this perspective gives us the means of understanding and working with archetypes in different ways. But regardless of how they came into existence, through evolution or design, the fact remains that these archetypes presently exist in the collective unconscious, and so we must take account of them in our life. To not do so would be extremely naïve. We would then simply have these forces operating within us without our understanding of what is happening. The archetypes are active parts of the game, and we learn to work with them.

COMING INTO RELATIONSHIP WITH OUR SUBCONSCIOUS

We need to stop for a moment and catch our breath. It might seem complicated; light shadow, dark shadow, collective unconscious, archetypes, all operating within us, but this is who we are and how we work. Fortunately these aspects of ourselves all come together in a synchronistic way as we progress along the path. These different parts naturally align themselves as we practice our quantum techniques and move towards awakening. The path of self-knowledge, once embarked upon, opens many doors. Our relationship with our subconscious will grow and mature as we spend time with it.

We begin by dialoguing with our subconscious. We call it by its mythic titles, building familiarity with it and reminding ourselves of its functions and powers, its ability to help us. We welcome back this forgotten and neglected part of ourselves, like we would a long-lost brother. We appreciate the unique role our subconscious plays in our life, and we resolve to give it very clear patterns and instructions, so that we can work together as a team. We contemplate the quantum maxims, and our understanding of the subconscious and the energy web grows, giving us clarity as to what roles they play in our life. We become familiar with our patterns and begin to discover our shadow parts, integrating them into our lives. In all these ways we build our relationship with our subconscious.

I began my relationship with my subconscious many years ago by repeating a very simple affirmation, "My subconscious mind is my partner in success." I have repeated this affirmation to myself thousands of times over the years, and so it has been imprinted and is now a resonating force within me.

This practice had great value for me. Firstly, by affirming "my subconscious mind," I was reminding my conscious mind of the existence of this second mind. Our mind must be reminded many times of the existence of this incredible part of us, or else the subconscious is mostly forgotten and ignored by the mind. By adding the words "my partner," I was also educating the conscious mind as to the possibilities and advantages of working with the subconscious. I was letting my mind know it had a partner who was willing and anxious to work with it, that it did not need to work alone. And finally, by using the word "success," I was building up a success vibration, weaving the image of success into my subconscious.

Now in working with a warrior mythology, I've changed this affirmation slightly. Instead of saying "my" subconscious mind I say, "Our subconscious mind is our partner in success." When the affirmation becomes "our subconscious," the mind must momentarily think, "Who is 'our' referring to?" The affirmation reminds the mind that we have both the body and the soul, and that they have the subconscious as their partner. It's a subtle but important difference, and now every time I use the new affirmation I am thinking about these other parts of myself as well. I ask myself, "What patterns am I weaving for my body?" and "What patterns am I weaving for my soul?" Working with the subconscious is creative work, and we become artists creating our own reality. Now that we have discovered our "partner in success," we use this partner in every area of our life, continually deepening our relationship with it.

Finally, in subconscious work we listen to our dreams, notice omens, trust and act upon our gut instincts. We are forever vigilant, conscious of whatever is communicating with us. We trust this type of knowing, understanding that it does not come from the mind but from the other parts of us. This is what we call 'listening', and it is a crucial part of coming into relationship with our subconscious. Listening becomes a part of our daily practice. In the following chapter we will explore the different ways of listening and how we bring these practices into our life. In all these ways we honour and connect with our subconscious. As warriors it is a momentous occasion when we have our conscious and subconscious minds functioning together as a team. Now we have something very powerful to work with, and we are progressing well on our path to becoming an integrated human being.

NINE

Listening

"Chance is always powerful.
Let your hook be always cast.
In the pool where you least expect it,
there will be a fish."
{ Ovid }

African novelist Ahmadou Kourouma said it well: "It is not always true that great events can be read in the dawn that heralds them."[1] And he was right. We never know what each new day will bring. The most extraordinary and unexpected experiences surprise us with their arrival. Life is a mysterious stream, and none of us ever knows exactly where it will carry us. So it came as a complete surprise to me when, one evening without warning, my inner voice spoke clearly to me, "Close this chapter of your life. There is something more for you." I was particularly puzzled by this request because I saw no reason to change anything in my life. Everything was working so well. My career was in high gear. I was drawing large crowds to my talks, often in excess of a thousand at a time. I was making lots of money. My books were selling well, hitting bestseller lists around the world. There were more speaking engagements than I could handle, which gave me the luxury of choosing the ones that sounded most interesting. People were benefiting immensely, lives were being changed, I was doing what I loved, and I was taking lots of time off too. It made no sense to give all this up, but the voice was very clear in what it wanted, so how could I refuse?

Some people think it takes a lot of courage to follow the inner voice, not knowing where it is leading, but I disagree. It would take far more courage to not follow it. We follow it because we trust its wisdom. It has led us before. To not follow it would mean missing out on whatever adventures it is offering.

Each major decision we make in life is like being at a crossroads where two paths lie before us. It becomes not only the path taken but the path not taken as well. We cannot take both paths, and each leads to a different destiny. It was an easy decision. I gave up what was comfortable, successful and working well for something that was mysterious and unknown. It was a no-brainer.

The following morning, after speaking to my wife, we decided that I would continue to honour all the speaking commitments that were already booked but not book any new ones, and when these talks were finished I would take a two-year sabbatical. Since I had bookings for almost a year in advance, my radical decision "to close this chapter of my life" was more abstract than real at that point, and my life continued on more or less the same as it always had. However, the months went by and as my final speaking date drew closer I was becoming excited about what might unfold.

Friends and associates began learning about this upcoming sabbatical and the most common question I was asked, and I was asked it a lot, was "What are you going to do on your sabbatical?" My answer was always the same, "I'm going to listen." Curiously I didn't know quite what that meant, but somehow it felt right so it became my standard answer. Somehow my sabbatical was turning into a "listening sabbatical," which was fine with me, whatever a listening sabbatical might be.

My final seminar was a five-day intensive workshop in South Africa. I was cofacilitating with psychologist David Feinstein. David had asked me previously if he could bring playwright and singer Ann Mortifee to the workshop to add another dimension to the event. While I had never met her, I was aware that Ann was a respected artist, so I readily agreed. The workshop was a resounding success, and more meaningful than usual, this being my last seminar.

The following evening we met for dinner. My wife Sylvia, David, "Annie" and I sat around the table, a bottle of fine wine was uncorked and toasts followed. I was in a festive mood, remarking that this was the very first day of my two-year sabbatical.

"What are you going to do on your sabbatical?" Annie asked.

"I'm going to listen," I replied, going on to describe my twenty-five years teaching mind power, and how effective it had been in helping people to manifest their goals. "I'm really good at manifesting," I added.

"How interesting!" Annie replied, "I'm really good at listening. In fact I'm just coming out of a long and deep listening period, and I'd like to come back and begin manifesting for the world."

We looked at one another curiously for a moment, without saying a word. It seemed so unusual that we should meet each other at this particular crossroads in our lives, meeting at a point where each of us was going in the direction the other was leaving, with both of us masters in our own specialty.

"I could teach you manifesting," I said, breaking the silence.

"I could teach you listening," she replied without missing a beat, and again we just looked at each other curiously. Then, without knowing what we were doing, we leapt up from our chairs and began laughing and hugging each other. Catching ourselves, we sat back down, wondering what had caused such a spontaneous reaction. This happened at least half a dozen more times throughout the evening. We would be having a conversation, and suddenly Annie and I would be up from the table hugging and laughing and then catching ourselves, sitting down again, wondering what was prompting us to do such a thing. It was very strange, no less for David and Sylvia, who had no idea why this was happening either. It was as if our souls knew something we did not and were celebrating our finding one another.

So began one of the most remarkable experiences of my life. That evening we decided to mentor each other. I would teach Annie manifesting and she would teach me listening. Each of us would be both teacher and student to the other. Neither of us knew at the time that this mentorship would radically change each of our lives, leading us deep into mysteries we could never have imagined, but that's often how life works when you trust and act upon what calls you. It was also not lost on me that on the very first day of my two-year listening sabbatical I had attracted a teacher to mentor me into the deeper realms of listening. The very first day! When something like this occurs you take notice. There was something at work here beyond just luck, even though, as you already know, I am very lucky. This was an omen of things to come; at least that is the way I chose to see it.

Let me share with you a trick that quantum warriors use effectively. I could have chosen to see this incident in many different ways, including that it meant nothing at all. Each of these possible interpretations would be valid, and no one can say definitively which would be the most accurate reading. But part of building a powerful model of reality for ourselves is choosing the interpretation that best suits our purpose. To choose to believe that this incident was meaningless or a lucky coincidence would give me no power, even if that is what it actually was. To believe that it was an omen, a sign of great things to come activates something different. It resonates a different vibrational frequency. This choice is a silent acknowledgement to the matrix saying, "I see you working in my life." It shows that we notice and are aware, or, at the very minimum, it sets up a placebo belief.

Framing the incident in this way is a very powerful thing to do. My subconscious takes notice of how I am interpreting this incident. The energy web also registers my reaction and vibrates in response. This interpretation is affirming my connection with the web and showing that my connection is functioning, which nourishes me and gives me confidence. So with all the possible interpretations that this chance meeting might hold, I chose the one that serves me best. On top of this, I will add more power to the choice by regularly contemplating the significance of this meeting, affirming my connection to the web and using this incident as a source of power. Warriors take advantage of every opportunity to deepen their connection with life and build a magical model of reality for themselves. We are not naïve or living an illusion; we know exactly what we are doing and we do it because we can.

The first lesson Annie taught me was that we are in relationship with everything. "Everything is alive," she began, "and you must learn to discern and listen to everything that is being said by this vast lifeforce. When you listen with intention, listen with yearning, and are willing to get out of your mind, remarkable things will be revealed to you."

The "out of your mind" part of what she said caught my attention, for all my life I had used my mind to get what I wanted, and now Annie was saying to get out of my mind.

"The mind can take you only so far," she continued. "It has remarkable abilities, but it is also limited to its own dimension. Explore other parts of yourself like your body and your soul. They have secrets to share. To listen deeply you must listen to all parts of yourself." As I was about to discover, Annie was more than just an artist; she was an authentic mystic as well. She had taken the journey within, going, as she described it, "deep within all parts of myself."

For two years we met once a month for three or four days and instructed each other. There was no agenda or curriculum; we just got together and did what felt right. Through this process I deepened my ability to listen and awakened my body, and Annie learned the secrets of manifesting.

BODY WISDOM

The Hermetic tradition refers to the body as "condensed wisdom."[2] The body has its own wisdom and ways of knowing, ways that are separate and distinct from those of the mind. The mind thinks; the body feels. From these different sources we obtain two different ways of knowing. Just as the eyes see and the ears hear, and from these two senses we get different information about the world, so too with the body. It has a special and unique relationship with the energy web. Our body feels the world "energetically."

Unfortunately, western culture has forgotten about our body's unique way of knowing. How has this happened, where we have divorced ourselves from our body's wisdom, where the body's feelings are ignored, dismissed as unimportant or irrelevant? Our religions share part of the blame. Many religions dismiss the body as a temporary vehicle whose instincts and desires are to be overcome. There is a preference in spirituality for the transcendental, where everything spiritual is good and everything physical is to be conquered. The soul is elevated as the most sublime part of who we are, the other parts are dismissed as temporary, mortal. This kind of spirituality is neurotic; it leads to all kinds of problems. In this life the body is every bit as important as the soul, and both these parts of us are to be honoured and respected. It seems to me, from a spiritual point of view, that if God has put us in a body, it is probably not for the purposes of fleeing or transcending it, but rather to learn its mysteries, absorb its great wisdom, and to be nourished by this experience. Even from a practical point of view, if the body has wisdom and knowledge beyond what the mind can access, wouldn't it be prudent to tap into this source of knowledge? If the body does indeed have this ability, we are missing out on a lot by ignoring this part of ourselves. But does it?

Neuroscientist Antonio Damasio has done extensive research on the body's ability to feel and process information. "The body contributes more than life support," he writes. "It contributes content that is part and parcel of the workings of the normal mind."[3] One of Damasio's most curious discoveries is how the feelings of the body influence rational thought without our even being aware of the process. Damasio devised an ingenious experiment which he called the gambling task. It worked like this: Each subject was given four decks of special cards, and on each card the player either won or lost money. The subjects were told to turn over the cards one by one from any of the four decks. What they didn't know was that the decks were rigged. Two of the decks had higher payouts but more severe penalties. Choosing from these decks eventually resulted in losses for the participant. The other two had lower payouts but a reduced chance of losing, so the participant ended up ahead by choosing from these decks. On average it took most players fifty to eighty cards to figure out which decks offered the greater chance of coming out ahead.

Yet here is where it gets really interesting. Damasio attached electrodes to the palms of the participants and measured the electrical conductance of their skin. What he found is that after drawing only ten cards, their bodies understood which decks were the most advantageous to draw from and got "nervous" whenever they were about to draw from one of the negative decks. (He knew this because in these instances the body registered increased levels of electrical conductance.) The body figured out which decks were better much more quickly than did the mind.[4]

This extraordinary finding matches many of our own personal experiences. How many times in the past have we had a strong feeling to act one way or another, a feeling which later proved to be accurate? Probably it has happened to us many times. Intuitively we know that trusting our feelings usually leads us in the right direction. However, trusting our feelings takes on a whole new level of credibility when we realize that our body is forever receiving information, picking up subtle signals from our environment and transmitting them to us through this means. Our body feels information. The language of the body is our feelings, and the more sensitive we are to our unique body's signals, the more effective we become.

A friend of mine, someone who makes most of his decisions with his logical mind, (as many of us do) shared an incident with me that shifted his understanding of feelings. One evening he was with his wife, telling her how he distrusted feelings because, as he expressed it, "They distort the facts." His wife, a highly intuitive woman in touch with her feelings, looked at him incredulously and replied so matter of factly that he finally understood what she had been trying to tell him for years. "Your feelings are the facts," she replied.

It was stated so clearly, with such deep wisdom that he got it instantly. Our feelings are the facts! Of course they are the facts. What else could they be? They have no hidden agenda. We feel what we feel. We never doubt the authenticity of our feelings; they are as pure and as reliable as they can be. We may question our interpretation of what these feelings are telling us, but never the feelings themselves.

Poet Walt Whitman understood this well:

> I am the poet of the body
> And I am the poet of the soul[5]

Whitman knew from the depth of his being the wonder of the body. "The human body and the soul must remain an entirety," he insisted. "This is what I feel in my inmost brain and heart." Notice that this isn't a logical argument Whitman is presenting; he is "feeling" it. "I will not make poems with reference to parts, but I will make poems with reference to ensemble." Ensemble, what a beautiful, descriptive word! It expresses so well what we are: mind, body, subconscious and soul. These four parts of us are an ensemble, complementing and in relationship with one another. We cannot take them apart, listening to some parts and not to others. To do this is to have an incomplete picture of what is happening with us, for each part gives us a different perspective, draws from a different source. Each part of us is designed to inform and guide us, giving us different ways of knowing, making us complete.

Body wisdom is a wisdom that needs to be felt; in fact we can only "feel it"; it cannot be received in any other way. If we cannot feel we cannot access this knowledge. If we cannot feel others we cannot know others. We might understand people's motives and think we know them, but we will not really know them. Knowing people comes from feeling them. The same with ourselves, to know ourselves we must feel ourselves. We must feel what our body wants, where we are out of alignment, where our mind has chosen goals that are inappropriate, where we are being untruthful to ourselves. We learn to know what feels right and what doesn't, and to have the courage to act upon what we're feeling. This is what body wisdom gives us.

Curiously, even knowledge must be felt for us to truly know it. This is something many intellectuals do not understand. To know a truth completely we cannot just understand it with our mind, but must feel it with our body as well. A Muslim scholar once shared with me, "When dealing with the Qur'an, it is neither appropriate nor helpful to draw lines between approaches of the heart and the mind." All masters of Qur'anic studies have emphasized the importance of the heart (body) dimension as a necessary adjunct to the intellectual investigation of the meaning of the Qur'an. The heart possesses its own intelligence: "Have thy not hearts to understand," the Qur'an calls out to us, pointing out clearly that understanding with the intellect is not enough. And it is not enough. We cannot function effectively listening only to the mind. If we do so we become emotionally crippled, cut off from primordial wisdom. And cut off from our roots we become a distorted aberration of what a human being should be.

The mind learns to trust the mysteries of the body. It comes to understand that it is not alone, and embraces listening to the body. It sees the value of working together with the body, of having this partner.

The body becomes an exquisite living being unto itself, filled with mystery and wonder—something to be wooed and explored much like one would a new lover. The mind discovers a partner in the game. When this happens the body and mind become companions, each with their own strengths complementing one another.

We need to transcend our culture's petty descriptions of the body as thin or fat, young or old, attractive or unattractive—which is just needless chatter—and acknowledge how exquisite our body really is. Our body contains our brain, our heart, our skin; it lets us walk and eat and see and feel. It is with our body that we get up in the morning and approach the ten thousand things. Where and who would we be without this exquisite companion?

The mythic title of the body is "The Feeling-Knowing One in Time and Space." The body is all-knowing because it can feel rather than think, which is a more direct, pure connection with the universe. The title also has the phrase "in time and space," and this is relevant. Without a body there is no monopoly game nor is there a cosmic game. The soul needs the body to play cosmic in time and space, and that is why the soul and body have a special relationship. There are undoubtedly many different realities in the metaverse, and countless other games exist beyond the time-space frequency, but in this life we have bodies and they are an integral part of our journey.

The second title of the body is Navigator to our Destiny. We discover our destiny by following 'what feels right.' Our body knows at every point of our life what we should do, what is best for us. Only our body can reveal our destiny to us. We will never find our destiny with our mind, for it will always be distracted with other matters, and will always project its own agenda upon our quest. Our mind can try and figure out our destiny all it wants, but it is a futile attempt, for destinies cannot be 'figured out'; they can only be revealed and followed.

Everything in the universe can be felt by the body because everything is vibrating energy and in communication with everything else. People, trees, animals, truth, beauty, joy, even the subtlest vibration in the energy web can be felt when we are in tune with our body. Feeling beauty and joy, feeling others, feeling the pulsations of energy from all things—we have forgotten how to do this. These neural connections, pruned through nonuse, need to be reestablished, for when a person cannot feel they become one dimensional, handicapped in life.

A human being who cannot feel is trapped in thinking, though he often does not know he is trapped. This person prizes understanding and intellectual knowledge, moving from thinking to conceptualizing to judging, all inside his mind. He may be very well educated and knowledgeable, even highly respected, but if he cannot feel he will never know the wonders of the universe, and will be forever trapped in his mind. Thinking is prized by the mind and why wouldn't it be? That is its medium. Just as every parent prizes their own offspring over those of others, so too does the mind elevate the thinking process over all others, admiring itself for its cleverness and mental agility. The unenlightened mind deceives itself in this way, living in a shadow world of its own creation. It will not be cross-fertilized by the other parts of the self, and will, if not awakened, become "a pathetic thinking illusion," which is exactly what my body called my mind during an extraordinary encounter where my body had the opportunity to vent its frustration with my mind.

I must tell you this story. During one of our monthly sessions, Annie and I decided to construct a means by which my body and mind could have a dialogue. We both suspected that my body needed to be heard. We created an elaborate ceremonial process,[6] including psychodrama, where the mind and body communicated with each other freely.[7]

I should mention that one of our favourite sayings during our mentorship was, "Set the stage and the play will unfold." We were forever dreaming up ways to contact the different parts of ourselves. We approached our mentorship in an innocent, childlike fashion, wide open to whatever revealed itself to us. We also had another saying, one we would say to each other whenever something extraordinary happened: "Thank goodness we don't have a clue what we're doing." This might sound like an unusual thing to be saying, especially since we were both very skilled in transpersonal methods, but it demonstrated our trust in the mystery, and announced to the web our willingness to get out of the way and let the unknown reveal itself, without our trying to direct the outcome. We gave all the credit for whatever happened to the universe. Much of our time together was spontaneous and free flowing, working with whatever happened.

During the psychodrama process my body was extremely angry at my mind and vented its frustration at not being heard. At one point my body said to the mind, "Look at me, I'm real," as it danced around the room. "Look at how beautiful I am, and how I can move. I eat, make love, I can touch and be touched. I can feel, I'm real, while you . . . you are nothing but a pathetic thinking illusion!" My mind was shocked by this encounter. It felt exposed as it realized how little it knew and understood the body, and for a brief moment the mind envied the body for how extraordinary it was. The dialogue continued, back and forth between the two, until the body felt satisfied that it had been heard. This was the beginning of my mind's acceptance of my body as a fellow player in the game.

A disciplined mind which has entered into relationship with the other participants of self knows that each part has its own reality and wisdom. When feelings arise, the trained mind cooperates by stepping aside at the first sensation, allowing the body to fully absorb these strange and wondrous feelings. It does this out of respect, but also curiosity, for it desires to learn the enigmatic body wisdom that only the body can provide. It knows that unless it steps aside this knowledge will not come. Which brings us to an important point: We cannot think and feel at the same time. To feel deeply we must drop thinking, however briefly, and allow the feelings to vibrate through the body without the clutter of interpretation. These feelings inform the body with their unique language, and the body grows strong and healthy when allowed to feel and communicate in this way.

A Wallace Stevens poem very accurately renders the feel of deep listening:

> One must have a mind of winter
> To regard the frost and the boughs
> Of the pine-trees crusted with snow;
>
> And have been cold a long time
> To behold the junipers shagged with ice,
> The spruces rough in the distant glitter
>
> Of the January sun; and not to think
> Of any misery in the sound of the wind,
> In the sound of a few leaves,
>
> Which is the sound of the land
> Full of the same wind
> That is blowing in the same bare place

For the listener, who listens in the snow,
And, nothing himself, beholds
Nothing that is not there and the nothing that is.[8]

In deep listening we notice and listen to everything, and great are the mysteries revealed when we step aside and let the wisdom of the "nothing that is not there and the nothing that is" disclose itself to us.

We listen by allowing the feeling part of the body to feel. The body has not lost its ability to feel, but, because of the restraints the mind has put on it, the body has lost its ability to feel deeply. Through the mind's constant ignoring and dismissing of these sensations, the faculties have weakened. Considered unimportant and thus ignored by the mind, the neural connections that facilitate the sensations of joy and wonder have become dulled. Pulsations of joy, beauty and oneness are constantly reaching the body, but the body's neural connections have lost the ability to process or understand these messages. Through our understanding of neuroplasticity we can appreciate how this has happened. The original connections that so filled us with awe when we interacted with the world as young children were reinforced by the traffic they carried. As we gradually ignored these sensations, the circuits that carried this traffic were pruned away, and we lost our sense of wonder. By doing too much thinking and not having enough feeling, we have allowed awe and wonder to leave our lives. Fortunately these circuits can be reawakened and the neural wiring reestablished when we once again pay attention to the extraordinariness of life. Through simple attention we rewire the circuits that allow us to again experience awe and wonderment. And when these circuits reestablish themselves within us we will see and feel the world as it is, always was and always will be—miraculous, wondrous, filled with mystery and magic.

INTUITION

Intuition vibrates through the body as feelings. Our subconscious, in communication with the energy web, has access to all the information in the matrix grid and will supply us with whatever we require, guiding us in all our decisions through our feelings and instincts. Sometimes it comes as "the still small voice that speaks within," or as a feeling or strong urge, what some people call a 'gut feeling.' We are not limited to our five senses, but can be guided by what is commonly called the sixth sense. Apollo astronaut Edgar Mitchell has actually taken to calling intuition the first sense, since, according to Mitchell, "It has been rooted in the quantum world since before we existed." This explanation lets us understand the process at a deeper level. There is nothing mysterious about body wisdom. This is how we have been designed. We are hardwired to intuit, have gut feelings and hear the still small voice within.[9]

Some of us access all of these means while others have one or two that are more active, but each of us has our own inner ways of knowing. We have only to pay attention and listen. Embracing this inner way of knowing allows us to live a more meaningful and informed life. However, the word 'intuition' itself is a bit of a misnomer. Referring to it this way, as a noun, makes it sound like a wise sage. A better and more accurate description would be to think of intuition as a process, so it would become, "I intuited the answer." Intuit is in fact a verb, and so this is actually a more accurate description. We don't go to our intuition to get answers—we intuit, and through this process we access all the information contained within the matrix grid.

"I woke up this morning with the most peaceful feeling, knowing I had the job." This is what Sharon, one of my students, shared with a group of us on the day she landed a plumb job with an advertising agency. Over a hundred people had applied for the position, and though she felt she had done well in the interview, there were undoubtedly dozens of others who had done equally well if not better. Yet, upon awakening, something in her 'knew.' It was a feeling. Sure enough, they called Sharon later that morning and offered her the position.

The body knew. The body is constantly picking up signals from the quantum field. Sharon's body knew she was hired as soon as the decision was made. In Sharon's case what happened is this: The decision to hire her was made by a panel of four people the afternoon previous to her being phoned (she found this out when she showed up on her first day). Once that decision was made it became encoded and part of the collective unconscious. Going to sleep that night her conscious mind was very active, thinking about whether she had the job or not. While she was sleeping, her subconscious received confirmation that she had the job from the collective unconscious. When she awoke her body "knew."

DREAMS

Dreams are the intimate conversations we are having with our subconscious and our soul. I have been in dialogue with my dreams for over twenty years, and this unique relationship has deepened me over time. Often I don't understand what my dreams are telling me, but still I write them down, knowing that all will be revealed in its own time. Sometimes when I read my dream journal and look back at two or three months of dreams, I will see patterns I hadn't noticed, and suddenly I'll understand what they have been trying to tell me. Paying attention to our dreams is another way of listening.

A dream journal is essential for working with dreams. The dream journal becomes a book of mysterious wisdom cloaked in veils of symbolism. At first, as we record our dreams, only tiny clues reveal themselves, but the dream book will build from one dream to another, and we will eventually see patterns and repetitions, and a larger story reveals itself. Sometimes it will be individual dreams that "speak" to us, and sometimes groups of dreams whose patterns we interpret, but one thing remains constant—each dream is recorded in our dream journal, as this shows them respect.

Edgar Cayce, often referred to as "America's greatest seer," said dreams accomplish two things. They solve the problems of the dreamer's waking life, and they work to quicken the dreamer's new potentials, which are his to claim. This is what happens when we listen to our dreams; they enhance who we are.[10]

Whenever I have to make a major decision, I always go to my dreams for guidance. I practice a process called dream incubation. Just before going to sleep, while lying in bed, I repeat to my subconscious what I require. I will say something like: "Tonight I will dream and I will remember my dream and the dream will be about . . ." (whatever I am looking for). I will repeat this affirmation ten or twenty times, and then relax, knowing this request is being acted on. I expect my subconscious to respond to my request and it usually does. It surprises my friends that I go to my dreams this way, and it astounds them how accurately they guide me. But why should it be so surprising? This is what is supposed to happen.

Let me share with you several dreams which have guided me in the past. One was in response to an important decision I had to make the following day. I needed an answer that night, so I asked my subconscious to give me a dream, and it did, revealing to me what I should do. Without repeating the entire dream at length, the part that gave me my answer was where I saw myself being issued a parking ticket because I had parked in an unauthorized place. I was running to my car saying, "What's it going to cost me?" over and over again. Upon awakening, I immediately wrote down my dream and I gave it the title, "What's it going to cost me?" Giving a title to our dreams is another way of helping us understand them. With this dream to guide me, I then asked myself, "What's it going to cost me if I proceed with my plan?" In the dream I'm doing something I should not and being penalized for it, so I surmised that the dream was suggesting there would be a price to pay if I went ahead. I decided against the plan, which later proved to be the correct decision. My dream had helped me make the right choice.

The first dream workshop that I presented was also preceded by a dream which guided me. I was unsure at the time whether I had sufficient knowledge and understanding to lead this workshop. I had only worked with my dreams for a few years, and while eager to lead this workshop, I wasn't sure if I was qualified. I went to my dreams for guidance. In my dream I saw myself in a room where my hair was being measured by a group of elders, all with long hair. They were discussing amongst themselves whether my hair was long enough to be accepted. They had a ruler, and my hair was measured over and over again. Some of them thought it was long enough and some didn't. There was disagreement amongst the elders, but finally they decided that, by the barest of margins, my hair was long enough. I woke from my dream and after writing it down decided that this dream was telling me that, by "the barest of margins," I was ready to teach this workshop. This gave me the confidence to present the workshop, but also kept me humble, as I still wasn't a "long-hair" yet.

My two-year sabbatical became a three-year sabbatical in response to a dream I had one night towards the end of my second year. In my dream

I was climbing a mountain on an epic journey. I was two thirds of the way to the top when I met a stranger who told me that I must return to the valley before I could reach the summit. This seemed very strange, but intuitively I knew he was right. I returned to the valley. Upon awakening I pondered this peculiar dream. I felt strongly it was sharing something important with me. It was the symbols of "two thirds" to the top and the stranger telling me to "go back to the valley" which made me feel that my dream was advising me to extend my sabbatical. Prior to this dream I had been wondering what I was going to do, as my sabbatical was coming to an end. My dream told me to take another year.

Not all dreams are specific and easy to interpret. Often we are unsure exactly what they are telling us. So the question becomes how do we know the dream we had last night has anything to do with our request? It may or may not have anything to do with what we are asking, but because our subconscious is always trying to reach us, we can at least surmise that there is a distinct possibility that the dream has meaning for us. It is certainly worth our time to try to understand what it might be saying to us.

If we do not receive or remember a dream, we continue the incubation process until we do. We record all our dreams, noticing any patterns or similarities between two or more dreams. We approach our dreams like a puzzle we have to decipher, and gradually, with practice, we become more proficient, learning to speak the language of symbols.

THE SACRED WOUND

Sacred wounds are the personal crises that each of us experience at different times in our lives. No one is immune to them, nor would we ever want to be, for they bring great blessings and insights along with their grief and sorrow. Crises happen because something within us wants to be noticed, heard or paid attention to. Something is out of alignment, so a shift happens.

Sometimes it will be a financial crisis where we lose all we own, or a marriage breakup or a serious illness. Whatever the crisis, it always shakes us to the core and makes us examine ourselves, our choices, our lifestyle, our beliefs. Nothing goes unexamined during a crisis, and that is exactly what should happen.

Examining our life during a crisis, we see ourselves in a different way. Aspects of our life that previously had seemed so important and necessary suddenly seem much less important, even trivial. Other ignored or dismissed parts, with the razor clarity of the sacred wound, now become the most important things in our life. The sacred wound is always a call for shadow work. Something is calling to be birthed or sacrificed.

Crises are never enjoyable, but they give us an opportunity to take notice and "listen" to the cryptic messages they contain, and that is why they are called sacred. This is life's way of obliging us to make changes, for without change we stagnate. Comfort is the enemy of change, and we seldom make changes when everything is going the way we want. Our life demands change, movement, and if things are stagnant or too comfortable, we can easily ignore our deeper more important parts calling to us. Sometimes it is only a crisis that gets our attention. Crisis always precedes transformation, so we should welcome crisis when it makes its way into our game.

We can apply the philosophy of Phil Jackson, Hall of Fame NBA coach, who inspired his team during a very challenging series with these words: "The opponent is not our enemy; they are our partner in the dance." Reframing the tense situation in this way took all the pressure off his players; they could relax, go onto the court and play their best, which they did, eventually winning the championship. We should take the same approach in our life. Our challenges are not misfortunes; they are partners in our game. They are necessary parts of our evolution. They make us strong, lead us down paths we might never have ventured onto were it not for these opportunities.

The sacred wound is a necessary and valuable part of the journey of being a human being. It opens us up for something different to happen in our lives. We need to stop categorizing every event as either a blessing or a curse, good or bad, pleasant or unpleasant, and accept every circumstance as a way of deepening ourselves.

The sacred wound deepens us. In feeling our own pain we touch and feel the pain of others. We are humbled in a way that makes us search for answers. These times are never pleasant, but they birth new insights, changes, movement, both internally and externally, and we are enhanced in many ways. What seems like chaos is the creative alchemy of the universe pouring itself into our game, quickening us with its touch, leading us to our awakening.

LISTENING TO OUR LIVES

There comes a point in each of our lives when we realize that life is much more mysterious and magical than we had originally thought. Our life can no longer be confined within the rigid interpretations we have projected upon it. Unexplained, incredible things can and do happen regularly; this we now accept. Occurrences that defy our logic but make perfect sense from a quantum perspective are the norm. Our life is extraordinary and that is the truth. It is a magical journey in time and space and is forever communicating and interacting with us. We now know, our life does not just randomly happen to us, independent of who we are.

The events of our life always contain messages when we learn to listen to them. The circumstances we encounter can no longer be ignored, blamed on someone else or dismissed as good or bad luck. To think this way is to view ourselves as separate from the universe. We are one with everything; every event of our life has meaning. We trust this intimate relationship, reading the signs, interpreting the messages, open and receptive to everything that happens to us. There is wisdom in living this way.

As quantum warriors we have many strategies and the means to use all situations for our benefit. We have trained ourselves well in the art of living. Practicing quantum ways we come to realize something quite extraordinary; our intention to awaken has triggered something remarkable. The game suddenly comes alive in ways we could not have expected, and there are more players than we imagined. Now everything in the universe has the potential of entering our game. The web, past and future, people, dreams, events, signs and omens are all in "our game," playing and interacting with us in meaningful ways. Everything we come in contact with, we discover, is communicating with us, carrying a message, a blessing, a new opportunity, a calling, something that has meaning for us. Our life becomes rich, full, layered with nuances, insights and deep meaning. Our listening is awakening us and now we understand our place in the universe in a whole new way.

TEN

The Seven Disciplines

"Sow an act and you reap a habit;
sow a habit and you reap a character;
sow a character and you reap a destiny."
{ George Dana Boardman }

As we go about the ten thousand things that make up our life we vow to be our best in every situation. Being our best does not mean being perfect. Striving for perfection is counterproductive. It is unnecessary, neurotic and weighs us down with self-importance. Being our best means we give our full attention to who we are and to whatever task is in front of us. We do our best and leave the rest to the universe to accomplish. We trust this relationship and expect the universe to respond to our efforts.

We develop character, drop pettiness, train our mind, listen to our life and enjoy ourselves. Enjoying ourselves is not slackness, but rather an enlightened way of living. It is one of our disciplines. At every point in our life we are aware and active in what is happening.

Warriorship is living our life with a discipline. It is the daily practice of bringing quantum skills into our life. Discipline allows us to become our best selves. It gives us the means to awaken and live with integrity. It releases us from our pettiness and our inadequacies and gives us direction, a purpose. We have tremendous freedom in living this way, and so we build ourselves an authentic life.

It is in the everyday events of life that we develop our warrior skills and learn the secrets of energy. Energy is all around us, within and without. We learn to feel its ebb and flow. We notice how it leaks away when we think and act in different ways. Certain habits and practices increase our energy, while others decrease it, and we take note of this. We choose thoughts, beliefs and actions that enhance our energy, becoming alert, intuitive and able to act with clarity and precision. There are seven practices that increase our effectiveness, and we call these the warrior disciplines. Practicing these disciplines opens up an entirely new world for us, and through these methods we learn the masterful art of choreographing energy.

THE FIRST DISCIPLINE: STALKING THE INTERNAL DIALOGUE

The first hurdle we have to overcome is the restlessness of our own mind, and how unaware we are of the thoughts we are thinking. It is in these two areas where we really have our work cut out for us. We must become aware of how our mind is working when we are not noticing it. There is only one way to do this, and it is by *stalking our mind*. Stalking is a valuable warrior tool. We stalk our mind the same way a hunter stalks an animal. To successfully stalk a wild animal a hunter must become familiar with its habits, get to know its routines. Is it nocturnal, or does it hunt during the day? What does it like to eat? Where does it like to go? What attracts it or scares it away? Hunters will learn all they can about the animal they are stalking. We do the same with ourselves by stalking our internal dialogue to discover its focus. With stalking we discover where we are unconscious and how our energy is captured by dysfunctional habits. We stalk ourselves to know ourselves. Sounds strange? It is very strange. We are a complex creation with four different parts, each part with its own agenda, each part ready to fight for its territory, so this is tricky work, getting to know our self.

Our mind has many habits, and many of them we discover are not beneficial for us. For example, the mind talks to itself almost constantly. Listen carefully and you will hear it. It was shocking for me the first time I discovered the almost constant chatter going on inside me. I thought I knew myself, but I didn't know this about myself. We have become so used to the inner chatter that we often don't even notice it. Like the constant hum from a refrigerator in the room, we adjust to the sound and eventually don't even hear it. Stalking the internal dialogue is like noticing for the first time the secret conversation that is going on within us. It is the conversation we are having with ourselves: "The day is too hot, too cold, I need more money, Bob's an idiot, I need to eat better, lose weight, I wish I had more time, things are so expensive, I didn't like the taste of that, I hope the weather is better tomorrow . . . ." When we are judging and commenting like this we lose energy.

This constant talking to ourselves is a real problem. The internal dialogue distracts us, keeps us from being present. We confuse ourselves as our thoughts shift continuously, with no direction or purpose. Within any given day we can shift from being desperate to being ecstatic, and through everything in between. We can be happy, miserable, bored, upset, frightened, sad, disappointed and then happy again, all within a couple of hours, depending on the inner conversations we're having with ourselves. Living like this offers no inner stability, no place to find peace or rest in the confidence of who we are, no trust in the rhythms of life, no security in the laws of the universe, just endless thinking.

Discovering our internal dialogue reveals much to us. Stalking it over a period of days and weeks we detect patterns and themes that repeat themselves, and this is extremely valuable to know. Eventually we come to realize how ridiculous this constant thinking is, how utterly dysfunctional and self-defeating most of this inner chatter is. We begin to suspect that this constant internal dialogue is undoubtedly holding us back, which of course it is.

For most of us, it is a total revelation the first time we discover that we have an internal dialogue, an inner chatter that comments and has opinions about everything. Notice when it happens and listen to it. What is it saying? Is it positive or negative? What are its current favourite topics or themes? Is it critical of you or someone else? Who is it critical of? What sets it off? Does it have a morning ritual or pattern that it follows? When is it most active? Stalking and listening carefully reveals these things to us.

The mind's constant chatter has a hypnotizing effect on us. We become captive to our own thoughts, trapped in delusional chatter of our own making. However, while this illusion is not real in any absolute sense, our body experiences it as if it is real, as does our subconscious.

While our mind is indulging in endless chatter, the other parts of us are reacting to this thinking. If we are having an imaginary argument with someone in our mind, our body reacts in exactly the same way it would if we were having a real argument—it feels stressed and emotionally drained afterwards.

We also maintain our limitations with our internal talk, renewing them constantly with the energy of our chatter. Whatever weaknesses or hurts we possess become more entrenched as we repeatedly focus on them. Fears exaggerate themselves and find roots within, problems are magnified, relationships are strained; all based upon imaginary conversations and encounters we are having in our mind. Being captured by the mind in this way weakens us. The word "captured" is a mythic description of what is happening, but it is more accurate than not. We are not meant to live our lives captured by our minds in this way. This is not the way a human being should live.

Stalking allows us to truly see ourselves for the first time. It reveals to us our shadow parts, those aspects of ourselves that we have ignored or misunderstood. We see how certain habits like procrastination or lack of imagination keep us stuck in situations that do not serve us, and how our pettiness weakens us. After one month, if we stalk our mind regularly, we should be able to see and know aspects of ourselves that had previously been unknown to us. As someone who has stalked himself regularly, I can tell you that you will learn a lot with this practice.

Through stalking we develop a great respect for the warrior's task of awakening ourselves. We become increasingly aware of how unconscious we are, and understand for perhaps the first time the task ahead of us—to gain control of these unconscious parts. We also develop compassion for others. We begin suspecting that, like ourselves, much of what is happening in their lives is unconscious as well. We become more forgiving, and a spirit of generosity towards others develops within us. When this happens we know that we are on the right path, that the game is maturing us. With practice we learn to let go of all our judging, to silence the inner chatter and simply be ourselves with whatever is happening. This, we find, is a much more relaxed way of living.

THE SECOND DISCIPLINE: DROPPING PETTINESS

There is no time for pettiness in anyone's life, much less the life of a warrior. Pettiness weakens us by leaking away our energy. We must be vigilant in discovering our own personal habits of pettiness, and design strategies to eliminate them.

The first pettiness we watch for in ourselves is self-importance or self-pity, whichever one has captured us. Each of us has an inclination towards one or the other. Both self-importance and self-pity are the mind being overly preoccupied with itself. We learn there is nothing to be overly proud about, no matter how powerful, successful, rich or good looking we think we are, and nothing to be ashamed, discouraged or feel sorry for ourselves about, no matter how meagre or miserable we consider our situation. Dropping self-pity/self-importance releases energy that has been trapped in maintaining these self-absorbed positions, allowing it to flow into other areas of our life. Without self-importance or self-pity weighing us down we can relax, and simply be ourselves.

We also drop the pettiness of worry, fear, hate, criticism, or any other habit that depletes our energy. Stalking allows us to see our mind in action, and we can identify our petty habits. A half hour of worrying, for example, can leave us drained for hours. Not only that, but whatever we worry about we attract. Worry is focusing on what we don't want to happen, giving these destructive images energy and power. Why would we ever do that? Mostly we do it because we are unaware of the consequences of what we are doing. But sometimes we do it because we are lazy and don't want to take the effort to shift our energy. Many people are not prepared to change, feeling comfortable in their hurts, grievances, resentments, limitations—indulging themselves in these petty positions. Maybe we're one of those people. All of us get trapped in some sort of pettiness, more often than we realize.

Dropping pettiness means eliminating worry from our life. This doesn't mean we don't think about our circumstances and take appropriate action to change an undesirable situation. We're not being naïve by eliminating worry; we simply recognize that worry is always counterproductive. The same with fear; fear is worry taken to the extreme. Fear is a state that is extremely damaging to us. It cripples us mentally and has a toxic effect on our body. Fear must always be recognized in its early stages, with steps taken to counteract it. We can eliminate fear by training our mind to focus on the opposite of what we are worrying about. Fear can only happen if we are not vigilant, if we allow it to take root within us. There is a simple method that eliminates fear and worry. We begin by acknowledging that it is our own thoughts that give fear and worry energy; without our thoughts they cannot exist. This is a crucial point. Without the support of our thoughts, they have no way to sustain themselves. Just as a fire is extinguished when deprived of oxygen or fuel, we eliminate fear and worry by not giving them the energy of our thoughts. We focus on the opposite of what they are suggesting, and this takes away their power. Deceptively simple, logically sound and fundamentally true from a quantum perspective.

Let's be honest with ourselves; when we are worrying or fearful it indicates one of two things. Either we are lazy, refusing to give our mind proper thoughts, or we have no trust in the laws of the universe and see ourselves as separate from everything. It is impossible to have fear or worry if we practice quantum mind power methods and trust our relationship with the universe. We do our best in every situation, weaving the web with our thoughts, being proactive with our actions, changing what needs to be changed, and no more is expected of us. When we have done this we have done our best and can relax, trusting that, no matter what happens, the universe is unfolding as it should. This we believe absolutely.

Criticism is another petty habit we eliminate. Through stalking we discover that when we are critical of others, even in our thoughts, we feel weakened and drained afterwards. Do not think of criticism in terms of good or bad from a moral, social or spiritual point of view, though there are these aspects to criticism too. We simply notice, from an 'energetic' perspective, if it weakens or increases our energy when we criticize ourselves or others. The subconscious mind registers all criticism and vibrates it within us. If criticism becomes a habit, our subconscious will begin criticizing us at every opportunity, because this is the pattern we are giving it. Similarly, if we take the time to uplift people, see their positive qualities, expect the best for them, this too becomes a habit; the subconscious takes note and begins supporting us in this way.

It is our responsibility to watch for self-pity, worry, anger, fear and criticism—anything that weakens us energywise—and catch ourselves when we have slipped into this type of thinking. Every thought, belief and attitude we entertain has its own vibration, its energy signature that resonates throughout the web, identifying us with this vibration. We are responsible for whatever our mind is thinking.

Jesus knew how to shift energy, in fact he was a master at it, and his teachings reveal his unorthodox methods for doing this: Return good for evil. Love for hate. I can remember thinking, when I first heard this scripture many years ago, why would anyone want to do this? It seemed like a ridiculous thing to do, or at best extremely naïve. I reasoned that if you encounter evil you should overcome it any way you can, that if someone hates you or does terrible things to you, you have many options, but loving them was certainly not one of them. But now, with greater understanding, viewing these methods as a way of shifting energy, they take on another perspective. Suddenly it seems like a brilliant strategy. There is nothing particularly spiritual about these practices; they are shrewd ways of working with energy. It is a way of avoiding being captured by evil or hate. From a warrior's point of view it is an inspired tactical manoeuvre.

In fact most of the spiritual teachings we have been taught, when you strip away the dogma, are actually enlightened ways of working with energy. It is a good idea to revisit all the spiritual teachings we may have dismissed as unpractical, and examine them again with this new understanding. Applying these methods in our life has the potential of healing us, making us strong on all levels. In light of this discovery we need to revisit how we interact with others. There is obviously something here we have been missing.

For example, let's say we're angry with someone and have cut off contact with them. We might feel justified in this anger. Anger, resentment, hate and bitterness are always fuelled by righteous indignation, by events, real and imaginary, that we chatter about in our mind. We let this anger vibrate within us and are weakened every time we think of this person. Perhaps our internal dialogue takes over and we have numerous fictitious encounters with this person, all unpleasant, and each of these encounters weakens us.

From an energy point of view, forgiving this person would make a lot of sense, even if we don't want to. When we forgive someone, energy that has been trapped in the anger, hate or resentment is released and then can be used in other ways. Forgiving releases captured energy, strengthening us. The benefits of forgiveness always go to the one who is forgiving, not to the one forgiven. There is wisdom in living this way. When we drop pettiness we strengthen ourselves.

DISCIPLINE THREE: GATHERING AND HARVESTING MOMENTS OF FUN, JOY AND BEAUTY

We gather and harvest moments of fun, joy and beauty because doing so makes us strong. It is wasteful and disrespectful to not enjoy and appreciate the simple, everyday pleasures of life. It means we are either unconscious, neurotic, captured by pettiness or lost in our mind. We must try to be happy and enjoy our life; it is good for us to live this way. When we enjoy ourselves and drink deeply from moments of fun, joy and beauty that happen daily, feeling gratitude for these simple pleasures, we feel better, have more energy and become conscious. Fun, joy and beauty have never been considered energy sources before, but with our growing quantum understanding we see them in a new light. Everything, we discover, is energy, and gathering moments of fun, joy, beauty and happiness makes us feel more alive.

The universe encourages us to have fun. We know this because it rewards us with energy for enjoying ourselves. The universe encourages us to increase our energy by making energy sources pleasurable. Just as procreation is made pleasurable to ensure that the species propagates itself, similarly when we are happy, having fun, enjoying and appreciating ourselves we are rewarded with increased energy. We have always meant to be nurtured by these sources; we've simply forgotten our most basic need for fun and pleasure. We've become trapped in thinking, lost in busyness, preoccupied with other matters deemed more important.

In 2000, I wrote a beautiful book called *The Practice of Happiness*. Surprisingly, people kept misstating the title. They often confused the words pursuit and practice, and in speaking to me would call the book "The Pursuit of Happiness."

"It's not The Pursuit of Happiness," I would say, gently correcting them. "It's *The Practice of Happiness.*" We have been so indoctrinated by the notion that we pursue things in order to achieve them, that this Freudian slip happened time and time again, even though these people had the book right in front of them. But this was the whole point of the book; we don't pursue happiness; we practice it daily. Fun, joy and beauty are to be practiced.

Each of us takes responsibility for uplifting ourselves. We need not wait for life to change in any dramatic way in order for us to be happy. We harvest joy and beauty by enjoying the simple everyday pleasures that previously we had ignored or passed over. We make it our responsibility to be happy. One way we can do this is by the practice of appreciating what I call "perfect little moments," moments that contain fun, joy or beauty and need nothing else but what they are to bring us pleasure. We harvest these moments by abandoning ourselves completely to them, letting them fill us with pleasure as we experience them. Taking a bath, talking to a friend, reading a good book, falling to sleep when we're tired, gazing at the moon, hearing the sound of children laughing, enjoying a good meal, watching a bird in flight; there are so many "perfect little moments." We harvest them by giving them our attention completely, in the moment they are happening. Each day brings us a new crop to harvest. We practice fun, joy and beauty in our everyday experiences.

Living like this is a fundamental shift in how we approach our life. We take it one day at a time, one experience at a time. We give up all thoughts about having a happy and meaningful life. It sounds strange to say this, but actually it is an important thing to do. When we need our life to be happy or meaningful, we naturally get upset and disappointed every time our mind decides our life doesn't meet these criteria. A life is a long and intricate journey, so trying to make our whole life happy and meaningful becomes a daunting task, overwhelming when you think about it. But with the emphasis now on enjoying moments of beauty, joy and happiness each day we simplify our life. We live our life day by day, appreciating the simple things and being happy. Living this way nourishes us, and we are at peace in the simplicity of everyday life.

THE FOURTH DISCIPLINE: MINDFULNESS

There is one lesson above all else that quantum reality teaches us, and that is that there is only now. From a quantum perspective an hour from now is the same as an eternity away. Everything happens in the now. To the degree that we can live our life moment by moment, day by day, fully present with where we are we, we pierce through to the marrow of the greatest of all secrets: life can only be lived moment by moment. Now is all we will ever have. Now is the shimmering jewel of our existence. Mindfulness is the practice of allowing each moment of nowness, each day to be what it is, without needing anything else to make our life complete. We practice being fully present with whatever is happening to us in any given moment, embracing each unique now as a special unfolding of our reality. In the ten thousand things that make up our life, we play the game moment by moment. When we attempt to play it any other way we lose ourselves.

This approach is very similar to the practices of Zen Buddhism. In Zen each moment, each day is experienced directly, appreciated for what it is rather than what we think it should be. Everything that happens to us is a part of the universe unfolding, even the things we don't like or enjoy.

This living life moment by moment, day by day has a fundamental wisdom to it. Each moment is totally different from the one before or the one that will come next. If we are not fully in this moment it will be gone forever and we will have missed it. Zen Roshi Philip Kapleau said it well, "If we do not learn to perceive the mystery and beauty of our present life, our present hour, we shall not perceive the worth of any life, of any hour."[1]

Mindfulness is allowing the moment we are experiencing to be sufficient for us. Even unpleasant situations are accepted; for they too are part of our life. It is an enlightened awareness that allows us to appreciate the pleasures and accept the misfortunes, experiencing everything for what it is without being overwhelmed. Mindfulness happens when our mind is not cluttered with discriminating thoughts of good or bad, pleasant or unpleasant, but fully present with what is.

Brother Lawrence, a Christian mystic, enlightened himself by working daily in the monastery's kitchen.[2] He saw no need to go to the chapel to pray at the appointed times, as this he felt took away time from his kitchen duties. He felt God's presence in the kitchen as strongly as in the chapel. We too can live this way. We can awaken ourselves doing dishes, putting out the garbage, looking after the kids, closing a business deal, working out at the gym, visiting a sick friend; anything we do can be beneficial when we do it with awareness. We bring respect and dignity to every act we perform. Our occupations and daily responsibilities become means by which we honour our life's journey. Whether we are a waitress, a salesperson, a nurse, an artist, an entrepreneur, a student, a stay-at-home mom, a street cleaner, a company president; we use these activities as opportunities to awaken ourselves.

A valuable practice to include in our training is meditation, which is the practice of no thinking.[3] The goal of all meditation is to stop the incessant stream of thoughts that is flowing in our heads. This is difficult at first, but with practice we become clear and mindful in the process. Meditation also allows us to connect to the deeper parts of ourselves. I have long been attracted to the meditative practices of Zen Buddhism for the simple reason that Zen is the polar opposite of mind power. Mind power is thinking thoughts and directing them towards a particular purpose. The practice of meditation is to not be distracted by our thoughts but to experience life directly, without the filters and definitions of thoughts, opinions and judgments. Both ways have their wisdom. There are many excellent meditation techniques, and it is to our advantage to discover the one best suited to us and take this practice into our life.

The final aspect of mindfulness is always remembering who we are and why we are here. Each day we remind ourselves that we are quantum warriors with a mind, a body, a subconscious and a soul. We are exquisite beings of consciousness and energy on an extraordinary journey to awaken ourselves. As warriors we hold ourselves with a sense of dignity and grandeur, like a mountain or a giant cedar, and with a feeling of connection to the universe. There is no arrogance in this feeling, but rather a profound awareness of the beauty and wonder of the human experience. We respect the opportunity we have been given, embracing every new circumstance, small or large, exciting or terrifying, as an opportunity to awaken ourselves. All circumstances in our life are put into this context, and in this way we never lose our perspective about what is important and what is not.

THE FIFTH DISCIPLINE: DEVELOPING CHARACTER

Ultimately it is not just what we think and do that counts, but who we are. Who we are vibrates a unique frequency throughout the entire energy web. The universe cannot ignore who we are. Every quality we possess, both good and bad, resonates throughout the web, identifying us with this vibration. Who we are counts in the grand scheme of things.

Developing character is the practice of re-creating ourselves into the person we wish to become. With our quantum understanding we know we can do or become anything, so we free ourselves from our past inhibitions and take on the qualities that best serve our vision. There is no greater assurance in the wonder of being a human being than knowing we have the ability to re-create ourselves into whoever we choose to be. Whatever qualities or characteristics we envision, we can take these on through focus and practice. Courage, vision, creativity, discipline, generosity, faith, compassion—all can be ours, and more too. There are no limitations to what we can do. The discipline of developing character is a new creative skill that we use to re-create ourselves. A good question to ask ourselves is, "What one quality would transform my life in a meaningful way if I possessed it?" This gives us a starting point. No matter what our age or present situation we should endeavour to be the best self we can. Our light shadow contains all the positive qualities we have yet to become. They are within us, awaiting our attention to bring them into our life. It is both our opportunity and responsibility to let them shine.

I spoke previously of the discipline of dropping pettiness, but when we drop our pettiness what do we replace it with? Nature abhors a vacuum and will rush to replace whatever we eliminate with something else. This actually works to our advantage, as it gives us an unprecedented opportunity to replace our pettiness with the opposite quality, and have this become our new vibration. We eliminate self-pity and replace it with gratitude. We drop our self-importance and develop humility. We change worry into confidence, fear into faith. We eliminate greediness with generosity, laziness with self-discipline. We become proactive in changing who we are. It doesn't happen overnight or with a snap of our fingers, but it does happen when we commit ourselves to it.

We examine the habits we presently possess and ask ourselves if they serve us. Are they in our best interests? Do they help others? Developing character is a way of shifting our energy and becoming our best. We understand the potential of developing ourselves in this way. Our ability to execute on our best intentions and to do great things depends on who we are.

We should begin immediately to explore the energy possibilities of compassion, generosity, faith, and gratitude. Gratitude, for example, has a very specific energy that is extremely beneficial for us. In living with gratitude we uplift ourselves. There is a secret energy about gratitude that is not commonly understood. Whatever we praise and give thanks for will increase. Praise and give thanks for our friendships and they will increase. Praise and give thanks for good health and it will increase. Praise and give thanks for abundance and it will increase. Energywise, gratitude is one of the most powerful vibrations we can harness.

Courage, compassion, self-discipline, generosity, confidence, faith, creativity, resilience, all these have their own energy vibration and exist for us as possibilities. And much more exists for us too. We should weave the web daily with images of the qualities we wish to incorporate, giving our subconscious clear patterns to work with.

Developing character is not an abstract concept but a real-life activity. It is in our interactions with others, how we deal with difficult situations and the challenges and opportunities of daily life where we demonstrate who we are. By putting us in situations that call forth our best, the game always gives us opportunities to enhance ourselves. We need to be challenged in real-life situations to see whether our character is solid or not. We should not complain when this happens. It is through this process that we build character and make ourselves strong.

THE SIXTH DISCIPLINE: JOURNALING

Developing character, dropping pettiness, recording our dreams, weaving the web, imprinting beliefs; the warrior's life is full, varied, rich with possibilities. We train daily because we know the value of training, as we experience its results in our daily life. But always we are vigilant, on the watch that our mind does not trick us. We can never let down our guard, and so we journal to ensure that we have a clear understanding of where we are and what is happening in our life. In this way we do not have to rely on our mind to tell us these things.

The journal is an indispensable tool, as it keeps the agreements between our self and our mind honest. Without it we are sure to fall into the trap of not training. Quantum mind power can easily slip into a concept or philosophy, rather than a daily practice, and this we must guard against. Keeping a journal daily lets us keep track of ourselves. It shows us whether we are doing our exercises or not, and it is a place to record our insights, dreams and inner journey. Each week we list the exercises we intend to do for that week. We are very clear, writing down which affirmations we are using, which visualizations, what energy we are aligning with, what beliefs we are imprinting, what we are contemplating, what pettiness we are working on; we are very specific. We record everything. Perhaps criticism or self-pity really had a hold of us today, and so we journal about it. We record each exercise when we do them. We record our insights from our contemplations. This way when we open our journal we see exactly what we are working on.

I must warn you—your best intentions will be tested time and time again. Do not for a moment underestimate procrastination, inertia and lethargy. In my seminars I have a name for this tendency; I call it the Great Trickster, and our mind is indeed a trickster. Our mind is exceedingly clever at coming up with good reasons why not to do the exercises. Everything from "I'm too busy" to "I'm tired" to "It doesn't really matter whether I do them or not," and so on. The mind in its natural state is lazy, undisciplined, and not at all interested in "working out." Many times we must remind ourselves that we are not our mind, and face the fact that our mind will initially resist any attempts to discipline it. Don't think just because "you" have made the decision to practice regularly that your mind won't find ways to trick you out of this intention. The mind would much rather randomly think thoughts about whatever it chooses, as opposed to having a disciplined list of thoughts and concepts it needs to think about. The mind has always thought thoughts in its own way, with its own preferences, and this is how it wants to continue. Only through discipline, training and repetition of practices will we change this. Journaling daily becomes one of our most important disciplines, as it shows clearly through our entries (or lack of entries) how we are progressing in our training.

It only takes a few minutes a day, and by committing ourselves to journal daily, and following through with this commitment, we also build our willpower. Keeping our promises to ourselves is an important habit to develop. We might think it is possible to train our mind and do exercises without journaling, but experience shows it is not. We get sidetracked, and before we know it we're back in the habit of not doing our exercises. How do I know this? Because I've experienced it myself many times, and I've also had decades of teaching this system, so I know the common hurdles that novices—and experts too for that matter—encounter in their daily practice. Take it from someone who is proficient at this system, you need to journal if you want the best results.

Interestingly, here is an entry that I found in my journal recently: "Trust only the journal. Do not trust your best intentions. Do not trust the mind. Trust only the journal." Yes, I too get distracted and tricked out of training. This was written after a period of not doing the exercises. The entry says it all. We can lie to ourselves, but the journal will not lie. The journal cannot lie. The entries and lack of entries will tell us a lot. We will also discover the ebb and flow of our own consciousness, which is very valuable. Each of us has our own rhythms and cycles that would be impossible to notice if we did not journal. Like the tides of the ocean, our consciousness has its own secret inner flows, and with our journal we discover them and how they work in our life. As warriors we commit ourselves to be our best, and it is only through daily training that we can accomplish this.

THE SEVENTH DISCIPLINE: WEAVING THE WEB

In my workshops it is not unusual for me to repeat laws and concepts in several different ways, so the mind can understand them from a different perspective. Repetition is the key to neuroplasticity and reaching the subconscious. So we remind ourselves many times who we are and why we are playing monopoly and cosmic.

Let us start with first principles: we are quantum warriors and everything is possible for us. The quantum laws are our foundation and as we contemplate them we gain a deeper understanding, seeing clearly how we weave the web. We weave the web with our acts, thoughts, words, beliefs and intentions. What we focus on we attract. While these concepts may have seemed strange to us at first, they now seem so obvious. This shows us how far we have progressed. We contemplate the quantum laws and they become laws of power for us as we weave the web with who we are. We use quantum alignment to connect in consciousness with whatever vibrational energy we wish to use. We know how consciousness and energy work together, and we harness these forces to manifest in our life. All this is weaving the web and we should weave the web daily, as this is our warrior discipline.

These are the obvious ways, but in fact everything we do weaves the web. Developing character, dropping pettiness weaves the web. Uplifting ourselves and being happy; there is nothing that we can say or do that does not weave the web. Contemplating the quantum maxims weaves the web, feeling sorry for ourselves weaves the web, criticizing others weaves the web; we are constantly weaving the web by not only what we do and think but also by who we are. This is the great realization that everyone who practices these disciplines eventually arrives at. We are part of the energy web and are in constant communication with it. There is no moment of our life where we are not weaving the web. The web is being woven with our every thought and breath, and this is an astounding realization.

I mentioned in an earlier chapter that twenty to thirty minutes a day of mind power practice will produce extraordinary results, and this is true. This is what I call the formal practice of quantum mind power, but there is also the informal practice. Informal practice begins when we open our eyes in the morning and ends when we close them at night. Informal practice is how we think and act during the ten thousand things that make up our life. How we react when someone offends us, how our mind thinks when we're doing the dishes or driving our car, how we respond to the demands of others, how we integrate the lessons of the sacred wound; all these are informal practice. In this context our life is our practice and our practice never stops. Every moment we are called to be our best and live like warriors, even when we forget this and drop back into pettiness. Our life becomes a continuous practice, and we find great joy and freedom in living this way.

These warrior disciplines naturally shift our vibration, and this change is translated into every aspect of our life. We find, to our great excitement, that practicing these disciplines gives us increased vitality, mental capacity and grace. We notice that we are more at peace with ourselves, and that everything that happens to us has meaning. If we have life problems to work out (and who doesn't?), our increased awareness and vitality gives us the ability to deal with them. Our shift in vibration gives us a heightened insight, which is reflected in better choices and actions. As our vital energy rises, every part of our nature is quickened; we accomplish more, feel better and become increasingly intuitive and connected. We also find ourselves "in the flow," and there is a sense of aliveness that accompanies us everywhere we go. This is the path of a quantum warrior, and it is a good path.

ELEVEN

Quantum Time

"We all agree your theory is crazy.
What divides us is whether it is crazy enough
to have a chance of being right."*
{ Niels Bohr }

For as far back as I can remember I have had an unusual fascination with time. For some strange reason, the normal passage of time puzzled me. I was intrigued with how our experiences in life could just disappear into "the past" and not exist any more. My wife has heard me say hundreds of times, "And now it is in the past," referring to an event we had just experienced which now had somehow mysteriously disappeared into this void called the past, never to be seen or heard from again. I never knew why the movement of time fascinated me to such a degree, but now I know. Intuitively I had always known that time was different than what it appears, and I was about to experience the strangeness of time in a big way.

The first incident happened at a lecture hall in Vancouver in 2001. As I stepped off the stage, having just finished my talk, my inner voice said clearly to me, "Your investments are going to do well." I was not thinking of my investments at that moment, and the voice startled me both with its clarity and assurance. I walked to the back of the auditorium, answered questions, signed books, but all the while I was intrigued by what had just happened.

---

* Physicist Niels Bohr, early pioneer in quantum theory, commenting on a colleague's paper.

Let me fill you in on what was unfolding in my life at that point in time. Three weeks earlier I had made a sizeable speculative investment in several stocks that had gone horribly wrong. In three weeks I had lost over one hundred thousand dollars, and there was every possibility that I would lose more. Naturally I was concerned, but this concern was nowhere in my mind as I stepped off the stage. My inner voice has always directed me well, but what caught my attention this time is that it was confidently predicting the future in a very specific way.

What intrigued me for the next few weeks, as I reflected on what had happened, is how could it be so sure? Was the inner voice privy to what will happen in the future, and if so how? Has the future already happened in another dimension, and if that is the case then is everything predestined? What about free will? It was all very puzzling.

I continued to lose even more money for the next few weeks, but was strangely confident that all would be well. About a month later the investment stopped hemorrhaging money and began to turn around, and three months later not only had I made back all my losses, now I was up over a hundred thousand dollars. The voice had been right. It knew. But now the question became how did it know?

Time is so fundamental to our daily experiences that we resist any attempt to change how we view it, even though physicists have been telling us for almost a hundred years that time is something quite different than what we imagine. We still hang on to the Newtonian model of absolute time and space, even though this theory is outdated. We view our life as a progression of events, with one event following another, and it is easy to understand why we believe this, as this is the way it appears to our five senses. It all appears linear, coherent and happening in a specific order—one event following the other. And this is indeed what is happening in the dimension of time and space we are most conscious of. However in quantum reality, where we also exist as energy vibrations, physicists tell us something quite different is happening. As strange as this seems, in quantum time, past, present and future exist simultaneously and are interchangeable.

Time has always puzzled physicists, even the great Einstein grappled with the nature of time as he developed his relativity theory. According to Einstein, time is not constant and varies in different circumstances.

It all has to do with motion, and as objects travel at faster speeds time slows. This leads to the famous "twin paradox theory,"[1] which is often used to explain time's unusual properties. One twin goes on a space journey, travelling close to the speed of light for ten years, while the second twin stays at home. Upon returning, the twin who has been travelling close to the speed of light has aged only one year, while the twin at home has aged ten.

This time-dilation effect, first discovered by Einstein, has been proven through elaborate experiments using atomic clocks and hyperspeed chambers. Physicist David Bohm suggests that time is part of a much larger reality where sequences of moments happen, but not necessarily in a linear order. Time and space are relative, and ultimately projections from a different dimensional reality. If this is true, then everything that is ever going to happen in our lives already has happened in a dimension beyond our senses, and in certain cases the veils between these boundaries lift.

What probably happened to me as I had stepped off the stage is that my subconscious somehow broke through the dimensions of time and space, saw what was going to happen, and through my inner voice transmitted this information back to me. Either that or my inner voice made an incredibly lucky guess.

Prolific science fiction author Philip K. Dick also had an unusual experience where it appears he tapped into the future. In 1970, he wrote a novel called *Flow My Tears, the Policeman Said*. One of his characters in this book was a nineteen-year-old girl named Kathy who is married to a man named Jack. Kathy appears to be involved in criminal activity, but as the novel proceeds we learn she actually works for the police and is having an affair with a police inspector. Shortly after he finished writing his novel Dick coincidentally met a girl named Kathy who, as it turned out, had a boyfriend named Jack. Dick and the girl became friends. One evening, as they were about to enter a restaurant, she abruptly stopped, turned to him and said, "I can't go in." Seated in the restaurant was a police inspector who Dick knew—they could both see him through the window. "I have to tell you the truth," Kathy revealed, "I have a relationship with him."[2]

Somehow the events he was presently experiencing became the

146 Quantum Warrior: The Future of the Mind

material for the novel he had already written. Commenting on this Dick said, "Certainly these are odd coincidences. Perhaps I have precognition." It appears he must have tapped into this experience with the girl subconsciously before he even met her, but once again the question becomes, how can we tap into something that hasn't yet happened unless the future has already happened?

Now it gets even more incredible as I share my next story. During my listening sabbatical with Annie, we kayaked one afternoon to an isolated inlet where several months earlier we had a four-day vision quest. A vision quest is a ceremonial ritual where an individual takes themselves out of their normal circumstances, usually into a natural setting, and prays for a vision, a sign, an understanding that will guide them in their lives.[3] The vision quest had been powerful for both of us, so we wanted to go back and pay tribute to the place where it had all happened. After several hours of kayaking we came to the inlet where two months earlier we had spent four days together. We pulled our kayaks onto shore and began to pray and give thanks, when something extraordinary happened. It came first as a feeling, an overpowering sensation where I knew that I was not only here in present time but here in the past as well. I didn't understand what was happening but I knew where the sensation was coming from, and then I saw it. Like a shimmering apparition, half real and half mirage, I saw myself arranging my sleeping bag in the exact place I'd been sleeping two months earlier. I was now experiencing myself in the past. I have never felt so beyond time and space before or since. Were I alone I would have thought it must be my imagination somehow playing extravagant tricks, but as I whispered to Annie about what I was seeing I discovered she was seeing it too. We were both transfixed by what was happening.

Now let me be clear, these were not actual physical images of ourselves we were seeing. At no time did I think I could go up and touch Annie or myself in the past; it was more like an inner seeing that was somehow being projected into the time-space reality, almost like a quanta flickering between particle and wave. We watched in amazement as the images of Annie and I played out before us, and then we prayed. We prayed to ourselves in the past, guiding our past selves to the realizations that had yet to happen to them. We became our own guides from the future, mentoring ourselves in the past. After a few moments I said, "We must go now Annie." We were experiencing a dimensional shift and my body knew it was time to leave. We left the inlet and kayaked back to Annie's place in silence, each of us reflecting on the extraordinary occurrence.

Back in her kitchen we discussed what we had seen. "What did you see? What happened? Are you sure you saw that? So we both saw the same thing? What was it? How could this happen?" We questioned, challenged, went over every detail, still amazed at what had occurred. When the full realization of what we had witnessed finally sunk in, all at once we were lifted to another level of consciousness, and the beauty and wonder of the human experience flooded us with such intensity that we wept in each other's arms, then laughed and then wept some more.

My consciousness was at such a high level of awareness that I felt as if my circuits were suddenly overloading, and I found myself exhausted by the intensity of the experience. "I need to rest," I said, already making my way toward the guest bedroom. I lay on the bed, enthralled with this heightened awareness. I felt so clear, so aware. I had spent most of my adult life training my consciousness to allow something like this to happen and now it had. Then I made a big mistake. I became full of myself.

"Now I know I'm a magician!" I said to myself, filled with pride. However, the instant I said this, my enlightened awareness crashed back to normal consciousness. I was stunned. I felt exactly like a little boy who watches with horror as his scoop of ice cream falls off the cone into the dirt. Hubris is never a good thing, especially when playing cosmic. I got up and went to see Annie, telling her exactly what had happened. She laughed so hard that she fell on the floor.

This experience with Annie has forever changed my perception of time, opening up for me new possibilities of how to work with quantum time. I now know that past and future are one, not in a conceptual way, but in a real, experiential way. Experiences like this change the way one views the world.

While not a common occurrence, there are records of people having similar experiences. One of the more dramatic cases happened to two Oxford professors while walking through the garden of the Petit Trianon at Versailles. Anne Moberly, the principal of St. Hugh's College, and Eleanor Jourdain, the vice-principal, reported that while enjoying their walk, they noticed that the landscape began shimmering for several minutes, and suddenly they found themselves surrounded by people wearing eighteenth-century costumes and acting in a very agitated manner. Not only did they see this; they actually interacted with some of the participants. One man told them it was too dangerous to go in the direction they had been walking, advising them to turn around immediately. Eventually the vision disappeared; however they realized that where they had been walking just minutes earlier was now blocked by a stone wall.

Returning to England, Moberly and Jourdain searched historical records and concluded that they had witnessed the sacking of the Tuileries and the massacre of the Swiss Guards. Their experiences are recorded in detail at the British Society for Psychical Research.[4] While there is always the possibility that these two women concocted an elaborate hoax, the question becomes why would they do that? Why would these two highly intelligent academics risk their careers and reputations and open themselves up to immense skepticism—which indeed ensued—with no possible motive? The more likely conclusion is that it actually occurred.

The quantum possibilities this opens up to us are far reaching, and I now pray and visualize not just for the future but for the past as well. If visualization and prayer can affect the future, which we know it can, then it is logical, from a quantum perspective, to assume it can affect the past too. Who can say absolutely that projecting from the present to the past will not work?

But how, you might ask, could something that happened in the past be influenced from the future, since the event had already transpired before you began influencing it? Logically, if it has already happened, then nothing we do in the future would or could change that. This is true in time-space reality. But in quantum reality different dynamics apply. Here past, present and future are happening simultaneously, so while the incident was happening in the past, we would have also been in the future influencing it at the exact same time. Our influences from the future would always have been a factor in determining the events of the past.

Following this line of reasoning, nothing is stopping the devout Christian, for example, from praying for Jesus as he dies on the cross, since from a quantum perspective, this is not only a past event but is also happening this very moment. Could we from what is now the future be helping Jesus through his ordeal? Nothing is stopping us from trying, and if there's even a possibility that this might work, do we have an obligation to try? Could we also help Buddha become enlightened? If this idea takes hold, and millions of Buddhists begin projecting to the past to assist Buddha in his quest for enlightenment, maybe they were always a part of the reason Buddha became enlightened.

I still project back into the past to a motorcycle rider that I almost killed several years ago. It was a frightening experience for me, and it must have been absolutely terrifying for him. I was driving on the highway in a light rain, and I was in a hurry. I was behind a car that was going slowly, so I quickly checked both my rear-view and side mirror, then abruptly pulled into the passing lane. I had not checked my blind spot. The motorcyclist was just then in the process of passing me and I cut him off. I watched in horror through the rear-view mirror as his motorcycle swerved and gyrated wildly and he fought to regain control of his bike, at one point his handlebars coming within inches of the pavement. Miraculously he did regain control of his bike. Several minutes later, when I regained my composure, I began praying with my wife. We prayed from what was now the future to the motorcycle rider in the past, directing my attention specifically to the motorcycle rider seconds before I pulled in front of him. In my prayer I said, "From the future I am praying for you. A car is about to pull out in front of you. You must be extra vigilant and aware. Be cool. Be calm. You will be fine."

I was sincere and it was done with faith and intention. Did it work? Do I think that he heard my voice from the future just before I pulled in front of him? I highly doubt he heard my words, but it is distinctly possible that subconsciously something resonated within him seconds before the incident, perhaps a feeling that made him extra vigilant without him even realizing why. Considering I have now done this dozens of times, perhaps my prayers were the tipping point in saving him. I will never know. From a quantum point of view it is distinctly possible, and if it is a possibility then I owe that driver the benefit of the doubt, and so I continue to project to him. What is undisputable, now that this event is several years in the past, is that when this motorcycle rider was being cut off there was also someone in the future, the driver of the car, projecting to him from many different points in the future. These projections from the future had taken place.

Let me share with you another incident where I healed myself from the future. About two years ago I threw out my back and was laid up in bed. Now, I have thrown out my back several times before and my recovery had always followed a pattern. I stay in bed for several days, letting my back settle down and gradually it gets better. In a week I am back to normal. The body is a miraculous healing organism, and left to its own resources will usually heal itself. However, this time my healing was not following its usual pattern, and after a week I could hardly get out of bed. I began thinking of a good friend of mine who injured his back carrying a TV down a flight of steps and who has never recovered. Backs are like that, I thought, and I suddenly began worrying. And then I caught myself.

Worry only works one way, and that is to attract the thing we are worrying about. Knowing this I had to correct my thinking immediately, so I began mind power exercises to heal myself. However, I was feeling needy and vulnerable, and what I really wanted was to be looked after. I didn't want to do anything. I wanted someone to heal me, someone else to do the work. Then suddenly it dawned on me that I could call upon myself in the future to heal me, and so I did. I immediately began imagining what might be happening in the future. I imagined myself in the future singing, praying, drumming and healing myself. It was easy to imagine, but it was more than imagining; it was more like letting go and intuiting what I was probably doing in the future to help myself now. It was an effortless process because I didn't need to do anything; my future self was doing the healing. He was putting out all the effort. I didn't have to force this image; I simply imagined exactly what I thought he might do, and so I drifted into a reverie. It felt very relaxing and reassuring.

It was almost as if what wanted to be imagined, imagined itself. I simply relaxed into the soothing effects. I had found the healer I had wanted, and incredibly, it was myself in the future. I did this numerous times the first few days, and every time I did I felt my back tingling with energy. Now I was not trying to visualize or imagine my back tingling with energy; it actually was tingling with energy. Was it my imagination? Perhaps, but equally possible was that healing energy from the future was now reaching me. My back, which had previously not been responding, was now making excellent progress. In two days I was out of bed, and two weeks later I was fully healed.

Once the healing was complete I began the process of payback. I began healing myself, from what was now the future, reenacting the exact images that had spontaneously arisen in my mind when I was in bed several weeks earlier. I was completing the circuit of energy. When you work in these dimensions you must always pay back. If you borrow and access energy from the future, make sure you keep your commitment and do exactly what you imagined. What happens if you don't? You can never use this process with confidence again.

Did I really heal myself from the future? Was it placebo? Would it have happened anyway? No one will ever know for sure, but what we do know absolutely is that when I was suffering with my bad back in bed I was also simultaneously in the future healing myself. Both these incidents had always happened, just as imagined.

My protégé Robin Banks,[5] who teaches my mind power courses in Europe and South Africa, shares a similar story about projecting into the past. He was sitting in his steam room in his beautiful home in Johannesburg enjoying himself immensely when he remembered buying the house a year earlier, renovating it and having to make a decision on whether to include the steam room or not. There were many obstacles and challenges in fitting a steam room into the plans, not the least being his architect advising against it, and so Robin almost didn't, but he had this strong feeling that he should build it and so finally he did. It was the right decision, as he gets plenty of use from it and enjoys it enormously.

On this particular day he was in the steam room, reflecting on the decision he had made a year earlier, when the thought hit him: "I have to help myself make the right decision," so he began projecting to himself in the past. He said, "Robin, I am in the future. I am in the steam room and loving it. I know you are not sure whether to build it, but I am telling you that you absolutely must build it." He spoke with deep conviction and intensity, directing his instructions to himself in the past when he was struggling with the decision. He continued to do this for several weeks, every time he was in the steam room, and to this day Robin will occasionally project back to himself in this way. Could these instructions and guidance to himself in the past have helped him make the decision? Could these projections be the source of the "strong feeling" he had received while he was wavering on what to do? From a quantum perspective you would assume so.

I know this concept is hard to understand at first, but once we grasp the mechanics of it, it gives us another way of working with energy. We should regularly project back to ourselves in the past, helping ourselves in times of crisis when important decisions need to be made. In doing so not only are we helping and guiding ourselves in the past, but we are establishing important relationships between our present and past selves, and between our present and future selves as well. If we develop the habit of guiding ourselves in the past, then this means that our future selves are probably projecting to us now. I mean think about it; if we're in the habit of projecting into the past and believe that it is working, why would we ever stop? Of course we are being guided from our future selves. How reassuring, how empowering it is to know that right now we are receiving guidance, prayers, energy and assistance from our future selves. They are helping us because we have established a relationship with them. Our future self has an interest in us getting it right. Working with quantum time means the cosmic game takes, if you'll pardon the pun, a quantum leap. Now our future and past selves are also in the game, interacting with us. That is amazing.

When we practice these techniques regularly each aspect of ourselves, past, present and future, learns to count on one another. For example, when I did my "payback" to myself, I also let my past self know that it could always call upon me in times of need. I used these exact words, "I am your future self. You can always call upon me. I will guide you and assist you and do whatever you ask. Whatever you ask of me I will do."

I wanted my past self to know this, and so every time I project back into the past I let him know he can always call upon me in the future. This bonding between us gives me confidence when I call upon my future self, which I now do regularly. I trust, no even more than trust, I know my future self is doing whatever I ask of him. All parts of me, past, present and future, are men of our word and we trust one another. I have so bonded with my future self that now I know he is helping me without me even having to call him. My future self is actively playing cosmic and monopoly with me, guiding and assisting me from the future. How reassuring is that?

There are several scientific explanations to explain how this could happen. The most obvious one, of course, is the reality of past, present and future happening simultaneously in quantum time, but there is also a quantum phenomenon relating to retarded and advanced waves, the so-called Wheeler–Feynman absorber theory, which states that a wave can travel back in time from the future to arrive at its source. According to this theory electrons are radiating waves into both the past and the future. In quantum reality time and space are not separate from each other, but exist simultaneously in one continuum. So it is not such a stretch for consciousness to move back and forward in time. Even the prestigious and scholarly publication *New Scientist*[6] featured a recent cover story titled, "Quantum Entanglement: How the Future Can Influence the Past."

In an earlier chapter I wrote about the Jahn–Dunne experiments, where volunteers successfully influenced the number of zeros and ones in the REG trials. It was astounding to many that they were able to do this. Well it gets even stranger, and I have waited till this point in the book to tell you the next part. In 87,000 of their experiments, they had their volunteers attempt to affect the results, not while the machine was running but after it had completed its cycle. In these instances the random event generator created data in the regular way and, this time, the information was put into a sealed envelope without anyone knowing the results. Then, through conscious intention, participants attempted to influence the results between three days and two weeks after they had already occurred, but before the envelopes were opened. When the data were examined, the scientists found that the ability of the volunteers to influence the results after the experiment had been run was just as significant as when the machine was operating. Actually, this is not exactly true. The effects of projecting into the past were statistically greater than when doing it as the machine was operating. This is suggesting that our thoughts might have even greater power when projected into the past or future.

The possibilities of what we can do with this information are limited only by our belief in what is possible, and, more importantly, by our willingness to implement these new practices in our lives. We should regularly practice projecting back into the past and calling upon ourselves in the future. We should establish these relationships. Doing this has a subtle but powerful effect on the subconscious as well. The subconscious registers this strange and unusual practice. When projecting into the past and being assisted from the future is practiced repeatedly, the subconscious accepts this activity. At the very minimum it becomes a placebo belief and will work for us in this way. What is more probable, however, is that by doing these exercises, much like what occurred in the Pascual-Leone finger exercises, we are rewiring the neural circuits in our brain to actually develop these abilities. It is possible that these abilities will be normal functions of future generations as our species evolves into cosmic consciousness.

QUANTUM PARTNERS IN TIME AND SPACE

We can enter into a quantum relationship with anyone who has ever existed in the universe. You have already seen how I did this in calling upon my future self to heal me, and we can take this further if we choose. Why not align with and receive wisdom and guidance from the great teachers, the men and women whom we most admire and wish to emulate?

This ability was discovered by Napoleon Hill, who was mentored by none other than the great industrialist Andrew Carnegie, who at the turn of the twentieth century was the richest and most powerful man in the world. Hill learned the laws of success from this savvy businessman and became wealthy in the process, but it was more than just wealth and success he acquired. Carnegie, who understood the role consciousness plays in achieving success, introduced the young man to the means of tapping into his subconscious mind. Through Carnegie's guidance Hill employed a most unusual practice, which allowed him to tap into the quantum field, though he didn't call it that at the time. He describes in his book *Think and Grow Rich,* how he would hold regular imaginary meetings with what he called his "Invisible Counselors." These were the nine individuals whom he most admired and wanted to emulate.

His practice was originally designed as a way to "impress my subconscious with certain characteristics I desired to acquire." What Hill discovered in addition was that, as he spoke to them in his imagination, his mentors would in turn speak to him, giving him what he called "uncanny valuable information." This both surprised and startled him, "I was astounded by the discovery that these imaginary figures became apparently real." In fact, these meetings became so realistic that Hill suspended them for a while, fearing he was losing his mind. However, their value to him was so great that he soon restarted this practice and went to them not only with his own needs, but those of his clients as well.[7]

I have taught this practice to many people. One of the individuals I taught was Graham Kearney, a young artist of prodigious talent whom I met in South Africa on a lecture tour. Using this method he began having imaginary conversations with the great artists of the past. Sharing his experiences with me one afternoon, he was convinced that it was more than just his imagination. "I really feel their presence guiding me. They are with me. I know that." Something was obviously working for him, because his paintings now grace the lobbies of major hotels and the homes of wealthy patrons around the world.

Respected mystic Andrew Harvey describes having a quantum relationship with his *Rinpoche.* "Meditating on him, on everything he was and said took me deeper and deeper into him. I began to learn that by thinking passionately of an enlightened master like him at every moment, you could begin to enter his wisdom mind, and your own, and receive guidance and inspiration from his dimension."[8]

Jesus, Buddha, Leonardo da Vinci, Richard Branson; we can connect in a quantum way with these individuals. Great artists, brilliant innovators, savvy entrepreneurs, devout mystics, whomever we choose, we can communicate with them. It is not difficult. The hardest part is getting over how outrageous it seems, and here is where our warrior training comes to our aid. Having imprinted the quantum maxims, and now believing absolutely in our ability to do such things, it simply becomes a matter of choosing who we wish to connect with.

However, before we even attempt to do this advanced work, it is best to establish foundation beliefs that support the possibility of this happening. We must believe in these possibilities before we attempt to connect; and of course outright skepticism will nullify any possible effects. This is the advantage of training in quantum ways. We train ourselves to be able to function in quantum reality, where everything exists for us as a possibility.

We begin by connecting with our quantum partners, feeling their energetic presence vibrating in the web. Having read and absorbed everything we can on the individual, we can enter into a sympathetic resonance with them, having imaginary conversations together, where there is back-and-forth dialogue. It might feel somewhat awkward at first, and we'll have to use our imagination to start the process, but there will be a point when the imagination drops away and something authentic happens.

Another method which I've come to think of as a more powerful technique, one I presently use, is to enter into a high telepathic rapport with your chosen quantum partner, and simply download the information. In this method we are not just tuning in with our mind, but with both our body and mind, and we "feel" the connection. In this meditative state we intuit or download messages that transcend words. It won't be words we're hearing, but rather feelings of connection. We don't even need to know or understand what we are receiving, all will be revealed to us in its own good time. Once again our imagination starts the process, but there comes a shift when it drops away; we cross the chasm and enter into alignment with our quantum partner.

Again, it must be stressed that our ability to believe this is possible is crucial. This is not a naïve belief built on hope, but rather a belief nurtured and strengthened by our understanding of the laws of the universe. Everything exists for us as a possibility, including having quantum relationships. It is our faith and belief in these possibilities that allows this to happen for us. Faith and belief are powerful energy forces. Warriors are comfortable using them, and these forces open doors into the great mysteries for us. Brilliant author and psychologist Jean Houston described having quantum relationships this way: "A high level of possibility becomes available to you. You get energy, insights, synchronicity and you download their luminosity."[9]

In practicing connecting to our quantum partner and downloading "their luminosity" over a period of months, there comes a point where we feel their presence with us at all times, and at this stage the relationship ceases to be conceptual. Our mentor becomes our quantum partner. I am speaking from firsthand experience here; I have established quantum relationships in this way. My quantum partners are with me at all times, even when I am not thinking of them.

Many ancient spiritual texts indicate that the past, present and future happen simultaneously, and that time itself is the child of consciousness. The ancient Vedas[10] make reference to our ability to transcend time. In the Bhagavad Gita[11] there is an episode where Krishna (God) appears to Prince Arjuna before a major battle. Arjuna is troubled by the deaths that are about to ensue on both sides, so Krishna shows him a vision of the reality behind time, and in this state Arjuna sees that all death and birth occur simultaneously, that what will happen on the battlefield has already happened. With this reassurance he goes into battle.

In the Bible, Jesus tells Peter in the garden of Gethsemane that, "Before the cock crows you will deny me three times."[12] Peter argues that this will not happen, but sure enough, before the night is over it has occurred, and as Peter hears the cock crow he weeps, knowing that not only has he betrayed his master three times, but it unfolded exactly as Jesus had predicted. How could Jesus know this would happen unless it had already happened in the future? We must think of these quantum truths and not be deceived by the appearances of reality.

THE FUTURE

Mankind's ultimate destiny has been wired as a 'possibility code' within our neurological circuits from the beginning of time. Strangely, in quantum time the future has already happened. In quantum time our destiny as a species has already unfolded; it has been decided through our choices and the choices made by past and future generations.

Assuming cosmic consciousness has happened to our species in the future, which is our premise, nothing is stopping us from calling upon the brightest and most visionary in the future, letting them guide us to what we should do now. To those in the future, we are the early pioneers vibrating in their past. They can guide us into the future, helping us to understand what practices and beliefs will midwife this vision into existence. Their destinies count on us getting it right. They have a stake in helping us, so why wouldn't they?

Thousands of years in the future, there are those looking back at our times, knowing we are still struggling, unaware of our potentials but on the very cusp of birthing cosmic consciousness in our species. This is a critical juncture for our species. I'm sure there are countless of them praying for us right now, projecting visions and images from the future back to us, weaving the web in ways we have yet to discover. There may be temples or whole government agencies devoted to just this task. It is possible, no probable, if my vision is correct.

Albert Einstein said, "People like us who believe in physics know that the distinction between past, present, and future is only a stubborn persistent illusion."[13] It is a convincing illusion, backed by what our senses are telling us, but it is an illusion nonetheless, and we must remind ourselves of this many times. We now have ways of entering into time that our predecessors could not have imagined. What seems incredible to us today will be common sense to future generations.

TWELVE

Creating a Model of Reality

"We need a new vision of the
human being in the world."
{ David Bohm }

Through our daily contemplations we have come to realize our
oneness with everything. We have imprinted quantum maxims
into our subconscious where they now vibrate within us day and night.
We have seen and faced our dark shadow, and its power is no longer
unconscious within us. We have awakened our bodies and we feel our
oneness with each other, with the energy web, with everything. We
have journeyed into the past and future in quantum ways. Now we are
building a model of reality for ourselves, a chariot of beliefs that will
take us deep into the cosmic mysteries.

At a certain point in our journey we are faced with the task of
nothing less than the tearing down and rebuilding of our own
cosmology, both internally and externally. Now that the veils of *maya*[1]
have been lifted and reality has been seen for what it is, it is unlikely we
would settle for the old, limited-reality models we've previously been
working with. Most of our models are messy mixtures of imprints
gathered together from parents, peers, religions, and society, not to
mention the influence of our own dark shadows. To remain with these
models would show an incredible lack of vision, or even worse laziness
and indifference. This is the point in the game where we take full
responsibility for re-creating ourselves.

Creating a new model of reality is both exciting and daunting, as there is a dawning realization that everything is possible for us. Everything? Once again the mind struggles with this concept. It still seems so unbelievable, yet this is the truth quantum reality reveals to us. And if everything is possible . . . well, it staggers the imagination as to what we might or should do. For guidance we turn to the great cosmic warriors who have come before us; we seek what they have to teach, and in doing so we are amazed at what is shared. Before quantum physics lifted the veil, revealing the mysteries of our existence, the words of the great visionaries of our race seemed cloaked in mystic references that appeared unworldly, beyond our grasp. But now, with our quantum understanding, we can approach the great teachings anew, be inspired and challenged by them. I can think of no better place to start than with the teachings of Jesus.

If we are prepared to look at Jesus' teachings not as religious dogma but as instructions to future quantum warriors, it gives us a new way of approaching these potent teachings. The implications of what he is saying are overwhelming to say the least.

"The works that I do ye can do, and greater works than these shall ye do because I go unto the Father."[2]

Jesus is teaching us the ways of quantum warriorship. Not only is he telling us that we can do what he did; he is suggesting that we should do more, must do more. He fully expects us to do even greater things than he did. Should we believe him? Do we dare?

In studying the Bible through the lens of quantum theory, further passages begin revealing themselves. Jesus refers to his association with the Father this way, "I and my Father are one."[3] Since he has already told us that what he can do we can do, it logically follows that we can be one with the Father as well. From a quantum perspective this makes sense; not only can we be one with the Father, we already are one with the Father, have always been one with the Father and will always be, because everything is one. Any separation we feel is an illusion of our mind.

But Jesus doesn't stop here. He gets even more outrageous, and we are presented with something so unbelievable that it breaks the restraints of our logical mind. In sharing this vision he wants to break all our concepts of ourselves, to be born again into new realities. Here is the scripture that does it:

"Be ye therefore perfect even as your Father which is in heaven is perfect."[4]

At first the mind dismisses this as outrageous. It's impossible. But then there is a sliver of a thought that wonders, 'What if he is saying exactly what he means?' Could it be that we are destined through cosmic evolution to become God-like? Is this the cosmic plan seeded into the web from the very beginning of time, just now finding its way into the fertile consciousness of a species destined to be God-like?

In the Hermetic Gnostic tradition, this very idea is woven into the core of the teachings. Hermes[5] was an Egyptian sage whose teachings spread throughout the Egyptian and Greek world in the pre-Christian era. All the Greek philosophers where influenced by his teachings, and there are some scholars who think Hermes may in fact have been Moses, though this is only speculation. Because of the fires that burned down the great libraries of ancient Alexandria, and the religious persecution that occurred during the Middle Ages, where ancient manuscripts were destroyed as heretical, not much written material remains of his teachings, but what does remain is enlightening and controversial. The following passage comes from Book 11:20 of the *Corpus Hermeticum*, one of the cornerstones of this teaching:

> "Reflect on God in this way as having all within Himself as ideas: the cosmos, Himself, the whole. If you do not make yourself equal to God you cannot understand Him. Like is understood by like. Grow in immeasurable size. Be free from every body, transcend all time. Become eternity and thus you will understand God. Suppose nothing to be impossible for yourself. Consider yourself immortal and able to understand everything: all arts, sciences, and the nature of every living creature. Become higher than all heights and lower than all depths. Sense as one within yourself the entire creation: fire, water, the dry and the moist. Conceive yourself to be in all places at the same time: in earth, in the sea, in heaven; that you are not yet born, that you are within the womb, that you are young, old, dead; that you are beyond death. Conceive all things at once: times, places, actions, qualities and quantities; then you can understand God."[6]

These teachings are explosive. Daring in their vision, yet entirely possible from a quantum perspective. This passage can be meditated upon fragment by fragment, with great results.

A valuable practice is to take one phrase only and make it the total focus of your attention for a week. This meditative technique was perfected by one of the greatest Kabbalists of all time, Rabbi Isaac Luria.[7] He was known in the sixteenth century as "the Ari," and to this day is as respected by Kabbalistic scholars as he was in his own time. He would spend days and sometimes weeks totally engrossed in a single passage of the Zohar.[8] Through his will, determination and focused attention he wrestled great truths, passage by passage,[9] from the text. This practice produced extraordinary results for him, and will for anyone else who takes the time and has the discipline to practice these methods daily. Take these phrases for example:

> Transcend all time.
> Become eternity and you will understand God.
> Suppose nothing to be impossible for yourself.

Contemplate these phrases one at a time, allowing yourself to be absorbed in what they are saying, not once or twice but hundreds of times, and you will receive great understanding. I have done this and it has revealed much.

INVENTING OUR UNIVERSE

Creating a model of reality for ourselves begins with conceiving an authentic vision of what is possible, and then by imprinting new beliefs into our subconscious that support this vision. These new beliefs shift our vibration and resonate the web with the new truths of who we are. We examine everything during this process, discarding beliefs that no longer serve us, dropping our pettiness, purging ourselves of everything that does not serve our new vision. In doing this we are in essence re-creating our own personal universe. Our quantum maxim states that everything exists as a possibility for us, and since everything is possible the question becomes what should we do or become? How daring are we prepared to be? From an evolutionary point of view, if our human species has been gifted with these possibilities, then surely we are called to awaken our cosmic powers and use them to their fullest. To not do so would go against nature. Some of us must be pioneers, breaking the restraints, pushing the envelope, as Jesus, Buddha, Muhammad and the great ones of our race have done in their times.

But again the question becomes what do we dare to believe? Where and how do we start, and what part of us decides which beliefs we will adopt? We cannot leave this decision to the mind alone, for it will distort the process by pushing its own agenda, so we hold council, seeking guidance within. What does our body feel we should believe? Here we listen to our feelings, our instincts, our passion. Our body, holding the pattern to our destiny, will want supportive beliefs that help us achieve our highest calling. What will our soul want? Now a player in the game, it requires new visions and beliefs and a means of achieving its goals. Are some things nonnegotiable with some parts of ourselves, and who exactly is negotiating with whom? We know our subconscious will work with whatever patterns the mind presents to it, and weave the energy field according to these instructions, but what vision will "we" give it? And who is the "we" making these decisions? It is good to ask ourselves these questions, as it helps us to understand the complexity of who we are.

The conscious mind must mediate between all the parties and not taint the process by bullying through its own agenda. Obviously the mind must agree with whatever decision is made, for as weaver of the patterns and custodian of the will nothing will happen without its willing participation, but guidance from the other parts is absolutely necessary, and an enlightened mind knows this. An unenlightened mind, on the other hand, if left to its own means, could easily conceive any possibility, however self-serving, and weave the web with these patterns, even though they are harmful to the whole. This is of course exactly what is happening worldwide today, and why the world faces such problems.

If we are spiritual we might ask ourselves what would God want me to believe, or Buddha, or Jesus, and create beliefs according to this vision. If we have no spirituality to draw upon, we can equally envision ourselves as stewards of the earth or compassionate human beings who want to make a difference, and build our models according to our highest ideals. Each of us must find our own vision and be prepared to follow where it leads.

We trust our heart, our instincts, our inner-knowing, dreams, omens, feelings—everything that has guided us thus far on our journey. We do not need to see the whole picture to begin, the whole picture is never revealed; we simply act and trust and act again, and in this way we are led deep into the mysteries. Insights are revealed day by day as we trust and act in an authentic way, weaving the web with what we are shown.

The sixteenth-century mystic and alchemist Gerhard Dorn elaborates on this process:

"Through study one acquires knowledge; through knowledge, love, which creates devotion; devotion creates repetition and by fixing repetition one creates in oneself experience, virtue and power through which the miraculous work is done."

The miraculous work is of course the remaking of ourselves into cosmic beings. It is a step-by-step process with clearly defined stages. Dorn speaks of devotion creating repetition, and repetition creating experience, virtue and power. Repetition it seems is very important to Dorn. This is not surprising, as repetition is an alchemical process, a key that opens the door to our transformation. We must understand the incredible power of repetition and not be fooled into thinking a change in consciousness can happen any other way.

Neuroscientist Michael Merzenich agrees. Merzenich, described as the world's leading researcher on brain plasticity, explains that new functional circuits in the brain can only be achieved through repetition. His description of the brain is of something which alters itself with attention and exercise, almost like a separate, living entity. It is always "learning how to learn," and paying close attention, intensely focusing is key to the rewiring.

Research psychologist Edward Taub also discovered that training should be concentrated into short increments, what Taub called "massed practice." It was the short but regular practice, rather than lengthy but infrequent exercises which produced the best results.[10]

As quantum warriors we know that it is through repetition that we weave the web, imprint beliefs, contemplate and deepen our understanding of the laws. All our quantum practices require repetition; nothing of substance happens without it.

A sixteenth-century alchemist, a famous neuroscientist, a respected research psychologist and a quantum warrior all agree on this point: Repetition is the key to achieving noticeable results. This is why we train daily.

Through daily quantum practices we re-create ourselves by rewiring our neural connections. With quantum mind power, not only are we creating new visionary beliefs, weaving the web, and transcending past and future, but by exercising these new abilities we are also rewiring the circuitry of our brain, and in doing so we are becoming new beings. The miraculous powers and insights of the great teachers of our race, which seemed so beyond our understanding, are now within our grasp, and the methods to achieve this are clear. What seemed such a mystery is now being revealed.

Now that we know what is possible, the question becomes do we have the courage and will to pull it off? Here is where our devotion to a vision comes to our aid. Dorn speaks of devotion: "Devotion creates repetition." It is our regular inner work which leads to devotion, which gives us the will and strength to pursue this path, to do the inner work necessary to awaken ourselves into cosmic consciousness.

Dorn further speaks of alchemy, which is none other than a veiled reference, a cryptic code word which to mystics and spiritual seekers in the Middle Ages meant awakening the soul. With all the religious freedom available to us today we often forget that there was a time when the church ruled with an iron fist, when any practices that were outside the strict orthodoxy of what was permissible were punishable by prison and often death. For this reason those like Dorn who followed alternative methods of spirituality used the word "alchemy" to disguise what they were doing and avoid persecution:

"Anyone who has studied alchemy for many years, has followed the recipes and done the experiments with complete devotion and love and repetition, changes his own personality. Only if you transform your own personality into one which is magically potent can you transform the outer materials."[11]

To transform our personality into one which is magically potent is the mystical path of building the temple within. "Magically potent" beliefs are chosen and imprinted into the subconscious according to our understanding of what is possible and the particular vision that calls to us.

We must think deeply about the model of reality we are about to create, for whatever we create "in the temple within" becomes our laws, our truths, and in them we will "live and breathe and have our being." There are no restrictions as to what we can create, so we choose wisely, calling upon all the wisdom and experience we have gathered. This is "the temple built without human hands." Brick by brick, thought by thought, exercise by exercise we build our inner temple. We rewire the circuitry of our own brain with these practices, only this time we do it consciously, fully aware of what we are doing, and we do it with a purpose and vision. Creating ourselves in this way is the work of the visionary, the artist, the quantum warrior, and great is this work. To choose our personal laws and build our model of reality is the ultimate creative act.

THE SOUL

Now the final part of the self is awakened and integrated. Our soul is stirred and awakened through the myriad of experiences that make up our life. The ten thousand things are fodder for the soul. The sacred wounding, signs and omens, dreams, ceremony, prayer, weaving the web, imprinting beliefs, developing character, dropping pettiness, mindfulness; all these activities, large and small, stir the soul to awakening. This is the way the game has been designed, for without our soul functioning within us we cannot play the cosmic game with any degree of success. Without our soul awakened we will lack the inner vision necessary to play at these high levels. However, with our soul active within us, everything changes. Now we can listen within and be guided, for this part of us has fresh new ideas on how we can live our life. It now actively participates in the designing of our new model of reality. Our soul becomes a player in the game, leading us in ways we had not expected, and when this happens we know we are playing the cosmic game for real.

In Kabbalistic teachings, our first encounter with the mysteries of the soul is called *Tiphareth*. This is when the mind comes in contact with soul consciousness. The virtue of this path is called "Devotion to the Great Work."[12] The Great Work of course is the transforming of ourselves into cosmic beings, where we "see and know things" beyond the capabilities of the mind. Use of the word devotion is deliberate; this is not an idle, weekend-only type of curiosity, but something which now becomes the focal point of our attention. The vision of what is possible takes hold and our priorities change accordingly. Now awakening becomes our primary goal; all our activities are viewed through this lens, and the ten thousand things become the means by which we achieve this goal.

The first mythic title for the soul is Navigator to the Cosmic, which could equally be navigator to our true selves, our eternal selves. It is through soul awakening that the paths to the inner dimensions are revealed. This is a different game than monopoly and suddenly, to the mind's amazement (and chagrin if the truth be told), it discovers the rules and objectives have changed. While monopoly is a game of accumulation directed mostly by the mind, the cosmic game becomes a game of letting go, and it is mostly directed by the soul. It is difficult for the mind to accept and understand this change, for years of playing monopoly have ingrained the accumulation concept to such a degree that the mind tries to add elements to the cosmic game, where we try to accumulate or "attain" our soul. But this is not how it works at all. We don't attain our soul; our soul attains us.

Awakening our soul is letting this eternal part of us play the cosmic game in its own creative, often unfathomable ways. We give up the life we've planned in order to discover the life that is awaiting us. This is a radical shift for us and it takes some adjusting. The Bible says we must lose our life in order to find it, and in so doing we are born again in the spirit. The Sufi poet and mystic Rumi put it more dramatically: "Set your life on fire."[13] All these references speak symbolically of a major transformation. Something serious is taking place when we navigate into the cosmic led by our soul. It is surrendering to the unknowing, trusting that we are being led to our cosmic destiny. This new way of living takes faith, but not blind faith. It takes faith tempered and strengthened by our warrior training. With soul awareness we find ourselves taking a cosmic perspective and not getting lost in the details of our life unfolding. We feel ourselves shifting into something larger, wiser, greater, and this new feeling reassures us. This is the beginning stage of the awakening soul.

Our soul now requires fertile ground where it can germinate its cosmic seeds, and so we assist it. The subconscious, properly prepared, becomes this fertile ground. Here the conscious mind is called upon to participate in its greatest task yet. It is given a vision so grand and empowering that it feels compelled to act, for the cosmic game has awakened it too, in ways it had not expected. In fact the mind rises to its highest potential playing the cosmic game. This game brings out the best in the mind, since it is now challenged in ways nothing else can. It becomes a game of great mythic proportions, where concepts of eternity, oneness and dimensions beyond time and space are presented. Inspired, the mind takes up the challenge, and with "devotion and repetition" prepares the subconscious for the transition with the necessary foundation beliefs. Through toiling in the inner fields and seeding soul concepts into our subconscious, we become fertile and ripe, ready for what is to come. The cosmic seeds find dwelling places within us.

Our warrior training teaches us that, for us to awaken, all parts of ourselves must be integrated, functioning and working in harmony with one another. We must not focus on just one part, whether it is the mind or the soul. Often when playing monopoly we focus only on developing the mind and the subconscious, neglecting the other parts, and likewise when discovering the cosmic game we attempt to attain soul consciousness by ignoring the other parts, and this is a mistake. When we focus on our soul exclusively or prematurely, what we are really doing is fleeing life's challenges and heartaches, seeing this as a quick way out of our problems. This is spiritual immaturity, for we must integrate all parts equally. Until we have integrated all parts of ourselves and established harmony in the kingdom of self we will not get far in the spiritual worlds, for the dark shadows unattended will drag us back and cause havoc. Until we have done our work, trained our mind, awakened body wisdom and have a partnership with our subconscious, the soul will prove elusive. Metaphorically speaking, before enlightenment, do the laundry, clean the house and learn to make a decent omelet. Awakening the soul is never fleeing life, but rather participating in life more fully.

Buddhists, believing that all this talk of a soul is distracting and misleading, do not speak of the soul but of striving for enlightenment, and in many ways they have a point. It is easy to get lost in the dogma and vision of the soul, forgetting that soul consciousness is not an idealistic concept, but a means of living life in an extraordinary way. Ultimately, all the various spiritual traditions are about transcending our normal consciousness into something larger and greater so we can be of service in the world. The fruit of awakening is service to others, and this is how we can recognize soul consciousness in ourselves.

SOUL WORK IN EVERYDAY LIVING

In Zen Buddhism the various stages of enlightenment are sometimes represented by ten ox-herding pictures.[14] The ox represents our true selves, our awakened being. The process of awakening ourselves is often metaphorically referred to as "raising an ox." Awakening is the epic struggle between our mind and its delusions, and our true selves. The final stage of enlightenment is called "Entering the Marketplace with Helping Hands."[15] The sacred text reads: "The gate to his cottage is closed and even the wisest cannot find him. His mental panorama has finally disappeared. He goes his own way, making no attempt to follow the steps of earlier sages. He leads innkeepers and fishmongers in the Way of the Buddha. Without recourse to mystic powers, withered trees he swiftly brings to bloom."[16]

Clearly, something quite extraordinary takes place when we access this level of consciousness. "Without recourse to mystic powers, withered trees he swiftly brings to bloom," indicates that when we are awakened in this way blessings and benefits naturally follow, for we become goodness itself. We are the means by which the universe blesses the ten thousand things.

How much clearer does it need to be? How simple and yet profound that the flowering of consciousness in our species evolves to where our ultimate calling is to serve one another. Jesus summed up the transformation by advising that the greatest amongst us should be servant to all.[17]

SOUL–BODY

The second mythic title of the soul is The Awakened Heart. When our soul awakens our heart overflows the boundaries of self, pouring itself into all things. The awakened heart feels our oneness with everything.

The soul and the body have a unique relationship, and this special relationship gives us some insights into our soul. The soul and the body have been designed to be a functioning team, much the way the conscious and subconscious mind function together. The body knows our oneness with everything because it feels it. The awakened heart longs to explore others, to nurture others, to experience our oneness with others, and this offers a clue to the truths that the heart contains.

While the mind may conceptualize we are all one, it can never truly know this because it cannot feel. Not even an enlightened mind can feel, but the heart feels this truth intimately, and by following the path of the awakened heart we will feel it intimately too. Our heart feels, and through feeling loves, and through love the heart desires to serve, to "enter the marketplace with helping hands."

Jesus knew this when he said to his disciples: "For I was an hungred, and ye gave me meat: I was thirsty, and ye gave me drink. I was a stranger, and ye took me in: Naked, and ye clothed me: I was sick, and ye visited me." His disciples were confused by this, not knowing what instances Jesus was referring to. He answered, "Inasmuch as ye have done it unto one of the least of my brethren, ye have done it unto me."[18]

The soul's desire to serve is not some idealistic concept where we devote ourselves to all humanity, but rather the more messy and real call that we serve those in our own private circle of relationships, our in-laws, family members, neighbours, fellow workers, strangers, those whom we come in contact with on a day-to-day basis. Jesus calls upon us to love our neighbours as ourselves,[19] but this is not always easy. In our busy and crowded lives we often find this helping is inconvenient, and if it is "inconvenient," all the better, for it tests us, seeing whether we understand the new game we are playing. And if this is how we feel, we must ask ourselves, to whom exactly is it "inconvenient"? What part of us? Our mind? The soul? It is never inconvenient for the soul to serve and help others. When our soul awakens, a paradigm shift occurs and we change. We change not because we feel obliged to live differently, but because we feel our oneness and want to live in a different way. We see the potential and value of living our life in these new ways. We have a sense of what this new life would be like.

Jesus spoke of it this way: "The kingdom of heaven is like unto a merchant man seeking goodly pearls who, when he found one pearl of great price, went and sold all he had and bought it."[20]

Notice this is a "wise" merchant who is doing this. It is an exchange of something valuable for something even more valuable. This is an important point to understand. We change not because we feel some spiritual obligation to be a better person. On the contrary, we do it because we see the potential for us. It becomes a means of personal fulfillment. We see it as a way to bring greater happiness and contentment into our life. It is a very calculated decision, made out of self-interest, and we must know this if we are ever to make the change. Trying to make a change because we think this is what is expected of us is futile. We do it because we see great value in doing it, period.

We become like the wise merchant, making an exchange, but what exactly are we buying and selling in this exchange? We sell our old beliefs, dysfunctional models, our pettiness and everything that keeps us stuck and separate from the whole. And once these are sold we buy awakening, cosmic consciousness, a new life. We exchange our old life for a new one, and we do it because the universe is encouraging us to do it, offering us treasures in return.

Dōgen, the thirteenth-century Zen master, described this process as "home departure."[21] Not that we physically leave our dwelling place, our families, our jobs, but rather we leave ourselves. We leave our old, stagnant ways to take the journey to our true selves. Dōgen considered this home departure, which is the same as our commitment to awakening, as a momentous step. From this one decision the rest of our life unfolds. We are playing cosmic at the highest level when we do this.

In Kabbalistic cosmology it is taught that when the universe was first created the Divine Plan was broken into numerous pieces, one for each individual soul.[22] No one soul knows or understands what the whole Divine Plan contains, nor will it ever, but each soul is required to discover its part of the plan, to actualize it in time and space.

Our modern culture has badly neglected our soul, and this is not surprising, considering how the mass media programs us via "repetition" with the values of consumerism, setting us firmly on the treadmill of accumulating more and more things. Often we fall into this trap and are satisfied for a while. But the accumulation of things will never satisfy us for long. There will always be unrest, a hunger for something real and authentic, something more fulfilling. Until our soul is awakened we will always feel that something is missing, no matter how good the times. We can try to replace this feeling with material comforts, relationships, sex, drugs, money, adventure, but these trinkets cannot replace the soul. They are temporary fixes, and a deeper discontent will persist, for this discontent is none other than our soul calling us to something more substantial.

Our mind helps us on this journey of self-transformation, even as it too struggles to understand. Home departure begins a journey and we travel it step by step, day by day. This process takes time and we must give it the time it needs. We must be patient with the process. We don't get to understand or awaken all at once. We assist our mind in grasping these cosmic truths, truths which are not easy to understand. The closer the mind comes to understanding these truths the more it is led into relationship with the soul. We acknowledge every realization, no matter how humble. At this stage of awakening we do not transcend the mind, but rather use it to reach the higher realms. It has been well trained and now does our bidding. We climb the mountain of consciousness one step at a time, nimbly leaping from stone to stone, over pool and crevice, sometimes falling and losing our way but always climbing on, higher and higher, and through this method we reach heights unattainable through any other means. When the time is ripe the old mind drops away naturally, like a ripe plum from the tree, and we find ourselves with something new and extraordinary.

Buddhists call this new state of consciousness "dropping mind and body."[23] It is a metaphor of course, for we still have our body and we still have our mind. It's just that we no longer have our little mind with its self-preoccupation, but the great, flowing ocean mind of everything, and our body is now the whole world. The fourteenth-century Christian mystic Meister Eckhart echoed this transition with the words, "The whole world is my soul."[24]

This is the path by which the quantum warrior becomes a human being. The ten thousand things have awakened us. No longer captive to our pettiness and shadow, our four energetic parts awakened and functioning, we enter into the marketplace with helping hands. Where there is disharmony we bring harmony, sorrow we bring joy, pain we bring comfort, despair we bring hope. The old way of living in our mind and acting only for ourselves has dropped away and something greater flows within us. We live in Buddha mind, Christ consciousness, cosmic consciousness, and this is now our home. The cosmic game is complete. While there will be other games (there are always other games), this one is complete. We have awakened. In giving up ourselves, we have discovered that we are everything. It is indeed the pearl of a great price.

At this point of our journey our warrior mythology is dropped. Having arrived at the shore of our enlightenment, the vehicle that brought us here is no longer required. What need is there now of maps, models or teachings? This is why in describing the final stage of enlightenment it is written, "He goes his own way, making no attempt to follow the steps of earlier sages."[25] There is nothing to follow. We are now something entirely unique, something never before seen in the cosmos, and this is exactly how the universe planned it. The divine spark that was encoded within us from the beginning of time is now alight in the world. Body, soul, mind and world have become one, and we are nowhere to be found.

Now that the full possibilities of this path are understood, an important question needs to be asked. Do we really know what we're doing? Transcending time, weaving the web, imprinting the subconscious, choosing beliefs, discovering our shadow, the collective unconscious, creating new models of reality, awakening our soul, becoming a quantum warrior; it all seems so incredible, so we must ask ourselves how we know that we're not living an illusion by following this path. The short and simple answer is that we don't. But fortunately, we have a method to keep us honest and on track. We simply look at our life and ask ourselves, "How is it going?" Am I successful at the tasks I set for myself? Am I doing well? How are my relationships? How is my relationship with my spouse, my family and friends? Am I happier, more at peace with myself than I was before I began these practices? Am I becoming more compassionate and understanding with others? The answers to these questions tell us a lot, and we must trust what they tell us. Can we be moved with joy and happiness with simple everyday things, like the sight of the moon or the sound of children playing? Are we helping others? We can always trust the magic mirror of our life to reflect back to us how we are doing.

In practicing quantum mind power we should see positive changes in our life, in our relationships with others, and they should see these changes in us, notice our improvements. The Path of Warriorship produces results for our self and others. If we are not getting these results, or our results are not beneficial, then we must stop and reexamine what we are doing. Perhaps this path is not for us and we had best find something else. We always come back to our life. We trust what our life is telling us. This way we are sure to avoid delusion.

It is also important for me to share with you that most of the shamans, mystics and teachers I have known, studied with and often befriended over forty years have been ordinary human beings. They could be brilliant one moment and unconscious another. They were very much human, actually just like you and me. They had responsibilities, raised families, struggled with their dark shadows, made mistakes; they were real human beings. I'm sharing this with you because it is important that you don't think that the path of the quantum warrior is an idealistic concept, suitable only for the few. This path is available to anyone who hears its call, who is up for the adventure.

Perhaps the most valuable piece of information I have ever received was given to me by a Chippewa medicine man, Sun Bear,[26] one sunny afternoon as we were about to participate in a potlatch ceremony. It was not shared in any grand manner, and I doubt he had any idea how profound his words would be for me.

"A medicine man is only as good as his belief in himself. No more or no less. Each of us has our own bag of tricks that works for us. No two of us are the same. We each find our own path and live our own truth and that's just how it is."

Sun Bear, with these very simple words, revealed something powerful to me. There was no pretence or elevating himself above others or pretending he was something he was not. He was a simple

and humble man who believed in himself and had his "bag of tricks."
He was an authentic human being.

The term "bag of tricks" was an excellent choice of words, for it
takes what seems mysterious and simplifies it. It takes away what I
sometimes call "the stench of spirituality," the pretence and spiritual
arrogance that often infect seekers and teachers alike as they progress
within the mysteries. Each of us gathers together our own "bag of
tricks," whether we choose to call it this or not, "and that's just how it
is." Quantum warriors, shamans, mystics, Buddhist monks, successful
entrepreneurs, visionary artists, working mothers; we all have our own
unique bag of tricks that gets us through. Quantum warriorship is a
bag of tricks, no more and no less. Each of us chooses our own means
to navigate our journey. We get to be or do whatever we want. We have
free will to choose our beliefs, set our goals, and design our lives. We
can follow the path of others or forge one of our own. Everything exists
for us as a possibility.

THIRTEEN

Conscious Evolution

"We are moving from
unconscious evolution through natural selection
to conscious evolution by choice."
{ Barbara Marx Hubbard }

When future historians write the history of mankind's evolution in the twenty-first century, it is possible that this era will be seen as mankind's finest hour, the time of the Great Awakening, where cosmic consciousness swept the planet, changing everything in its wake. It will happen if enough of us choose it to happen and act in visionary ways.

The collective image each of us has of the future is what is creating the future, and from this perspective it becomes our social and spiritual responsibility to believe absolutely in a glorious tomorrow. We need visions radically different from the seemingly constant pessimistic financial, social and environmental scenarios that bombard us each day through our media. These dysfunctional images weave the web and create an energetic field that attracts exactly the outcomes we fear. If the collective belief of our species is in hopelessness, these powerful messages find themselves in the collective unconscious, and unfortunately there are millions of us weaving just such images without our even being aware of what we are doing. Each of us can take responsibility for shifting the energy in the other direction. We can no longer pretend that our thoughts and actions do not matter; if we believe this we are not warriors. Let each of us take responsibility to weave the web every day with the quantum possibilities of our species. If we wish to help the world, we can weave the web with our love, creativity, compassion, joy, generosity—with images of everything that is good and possible. Let's choose to believe that there is a glorious future unfolding for mankind and our planet, because each of us can believe this through choice.

There is every possibility that amid the seemingly unending day-to-day challenges and crises we are presently facing, another larger drama is taking place, the birth of cosmic consciousness in our species. As the cosmic game awakens us, new visions and possibilities reveal themselves. In moments of searing clarity, we know we are more than just husbands, wives, parents, lawyers, taxi drivers, sons, daughters. We suddenly understand that we are the sacred lineage of the human species, the stewards of consciousness, the weavers of patterns, the holders of all possibilities. The powerful consciousness that created the universe and which has existed from the very beginning flows within us, calling forth our latent talents, leading us to our destinies. Our personal consciousness, fed and nurtured from this cosmic source, is morphing into something else. A metamorphosis is taking place and we have only to let go and trust the process, allowing it to take us where we are destined to go.

The human race is a genius species with unlimited potential. While our history may be littered with wars, greed and injustice, it is also filled with compassion, generosity and greatness too. We have travelled into space and deep into the microworld of subatomic energy. We have transplanted organs from one person to another, cured many diseases. We have invented the printing press, the Internet, created great pieces of art and literature. Our species has an extraordinary history of innovation, creative action and goodness. This accumulated innovation and success is now woven into the collective unconscious, calling for more and greater things from all of us.

The code of conscious evolution, dormant for so long, is now vibrating within us, calling forth our talents and goodness. Our brains have been neurologically preprogrammed with cosmic codes designed to recognize signals from both within us and from our environment, and from the future too. If what I'm suggesting is correct, signals have already activated these hidden codes, triggering an evolutionary shift that is propelling us daily into uncharted territory. All this is happening while we are busy raising families, earning a living and trying to make happy and meaningful lives for ourselves. It is happening without us even noticing, but this too was prophesied.

The Bible speaks of the Second Coming, and from a strictly fundamentalist point of view this means the Second Coming of the man called Jesus Christ. However, there are also a growing number of theologians[1] who believe that this Second Coming is not of Jesus the man, but of the Christ consciousness that resided within him, a consciousness that will come "as a thief in the night."[2] The meaning of this analogy is clear. It will happen without us even noticing, which is exactly what is occurring now. Make no mistake, the next evolutionary leap on the planet is a leap in consciousness and it is happening on our watch.

A new thinking is making its way into the collective consciousness; it is busily weaving the energy fields even as you read this. The tides of change are upon us, and there are forces at play here more powerful than we can imagine.

None of us yet knows the role we are being called to play. Fate and destiny weave a mysterious tapestry. While returning from the moon in a space capsule, Edgar Mitchell, the Apollo 14 astronaut, had what he could only call "a mystical experience." As he approached the planet, an inner conviction revealed itself to him. He intuitively knew that the beautiful blue planet he was returning to was part of a larger, harmonious living system that he would later call "a universe of consciousness." Trained as an engineer and scientist, Captain Mitchell was most comfortable in the world of rationality. He had never before experienced anything like this, and this experience, along with the understanding that came with it, radically altered his worldview. He suddenly realized that, despite immense technological achievements in science, we had just begun to probe the deepest mystery of the universe—that of consciousness itself. Mitchell became convinced that the uncharted territory of the human mind was "the next frontier to explore, and that it contained possibilities we had hardly begun to imagine."[3]

Mitchell did not know at the time that this experience would lead him to found the Institute of Noetic Sciences and devote his life to studying consciousness. Often we are unaware of the vast impact individual events have on us. It is not until much later, when we look back, that we realize the significance these incidents have played in our lives. I did not know when I built my cabin in the woods some forty years ago that I too would devote myself to consciousness.

Each of us carries within us a unique piece of the cosmic code, a tiny piece unlike anything ever created before or that will ever be created again, and this is the wonder and mystery of the human species—each of us is called to express our uniqueness. The universe is prolific in sowing seeds of gifts, talents and destinies throughout the human species, knowing some will land on fertile ground and others on stone. Not all gifts will be discovered or expressed, and that's just the way it is. Even when discovered, not all gifts will ripen and mature. Our calling is our gift, and our destiny is ours and ours alone to express. Artist and choreographer Martha Graham put it this way: "There is a vitality, a life force, an energy, a quickening, that is translated through you into action, and because there is only one of you in all time, this expression is unique. And if you block it, it will never exist through any other medium and will be lost."[4]

Many destinies and gifts designed to help and enrich humanity have been lost by those who thought they had nothing to offer, who doubted themselves or had more important priorities, and our world suffers from this loss. Each of us should take it as our sacred duty to discover and share our gifts, our piece of destiny, no matter how humble or great we think they are. And how would we know how humble or great our gifts are until we begin to express them and see where they lead us? We have no idea where our destinies might take us.

THE ONE TENTH OF ONE PERCENT THEOREM

The powerful laser beam operates by creating coherence between light waves. Light is made up of millions of packets of light waves, with each light wave vibrating at a slightly different frequency than the one beside it. When you can cause just one tenth of one percent of these light waves to vibrate at the same frequency, that's one thousand out of one million, all the others automatically shift into coherence and vibrate at the same frequency, becoming a powerful beam. The required number for this to happen is one tenth of one percent, and this is how the laser beam achieves its intensity.

The reason I'm sharing this information is that it is distinctly possible that there is also a quantum number that applies to consciousness, and it may very well be this same ratio. If this is the case, from a cosmic evolutionary point of view each of us counts for a thousand. This is reassuring. It would be daunting if we thought we needed all or even most of humanity to think and act in these new ways before we could see a major shift in consciousness. But if, like the laser beam, there is a threshold number that is necessary to trigger the event of cosmic consciousness, then it becomes far more plausible that this could happen and happen quickly, even in our lifetime. If one tenth of one percent is in fact the magic ratio, in a species that now numbers around seven billion, it would take seven million of us to awaken in order to trigger this event. This is very doable. It also means that each of us counts for a thousand others. To trigger cosmic consciousness we need only one out of every thousand people to be inspired by this vision, to take up the path of quantum warriorship or a similar visionary discipline.

This shift will happen if enough of us come to believe that our personal awakening makes a difference, and we act accordingly. Individually, one by one, we must break the spell that has us thinking it doesn't matter what we do. It matters absolutely what we do. One by one we take our place and weave the web with our visions and actions. If we think it doesn't matter whether we contribute or not, this belief will stop us from acting.

This is more or less what is happening in our world today. Too many of us think that because we are only one person it doesn't matter how we think or act, but with our quantum understanding we realize this is not the case. Not only are we needed to step up and act, we need to step up and act in ways that are revolutionary. One tenth of one percent of us must hear the call and act in quantum ways in order to trigger cosmic consciousness in our species. Who might these people be? I think they are you and me.

What makes this vision so compelling and possible is that we don't need everyone to respond to make something extraordinary happen on the planet. We need only one tenth of one percent. Nor do we need to be Nobel laureates, millionaires, great artists, visionaries or even, for that matter, have anything exceptional to offer. We only have to be ourselves. Each of us is being called, so we listen within and act upon what is revealed. We act in ways that feel right for us.

I believe that this evolutionary leap in consciousness is imminent (in the next few generations) in part because of the crises that the world presently faces. Climate change, overpopulation, poverty, new strains of diseases, nuclear arms; the list of cataclysmic scenarios that face our species is almost endless. While it might seem somewhat counterintuitive, these present crises are hopeful signs, for the very reason that crisis always precedes transformation. These present-day crises, unlike anything the world has previously seen, may very well be the evolutionary awakeners that trigger the preprogrammed codes within us that will awaken the cosmic potentials needed at this point in time. It may be a quantum Darwinian survival of the species that is now taking place, only this time it is happening in consciousness. It is possible that our inner cosmic programs, feeling this vibration, are responding in the way they have been designed to respond, shifting us into a different level of consciousness, where we suddenly experience everything in a different way.

MEMES

Memes are seed ideas that organize our thoughts and give our individual actions meaning. The same way neurons build brain circuitry, memes build cultures and create common visions. Author Howard Bloom explains it this way: "The meme is a self-replicating cluster of ideas. Thanks to a handful of biological tricks, these visions become the glue that holds together civilizations, giving each culture its distinctive shape."[5]

A meme travels from one individual to another, from group to group, not unlike a virus spreading, eventually entering into the entire culture. Every culture needs a vision to give it meaning and purpose. When a culture loses its vision it loses its way. In many ways this is what has happened to us today. Our present memes—consumerism, self-preoccupation, getting rich at all costs, winner take all—are of questionable value, and yet we have inherited them from our culture and they reside within us as vibrational callings.

Typically each of us accepts the consensual cultural views without questioning or even noticing how this has happened. Up till now our memes arose more or less unconsciously, directing our actions accordingly. However, now that we are awakening we have the chance to see and understand ourselves differently. Now, with our quantum understanding, we can make choices to imprint revolutionary life-affirming memes that will foster a positive future for all of us.

The meme of conscious evolution is one such meme. The meme that each of us counts for a thousand is another. These memes could spread very quickly given the state of our evolving consciousness, not to mention the sophistication of our present communication systems. In this quickened age of instant connectivity ideas can spread at hyperspeed. A popular video on YouTube can reach millions in a day, fifty or a hundred million in a week. Facebook, Twitter, these new mediums give us the technical basis for unleashing new memes in ways our society has never seen before. It is not by chance that consciousness and technology are advancing together. There is a weave here too similar to ignore. The Internet is the technological equivalent of the energy web. They are both systems where we have instant connectivity and access to all information, where we are all plugged into the whole. That both technology and consciousness are evolving at hyperspeeds at the exact same time in our history is at the very least an interesting coincidence. You would not be faulted for suspecting that some type of synchronicity is at work here.

Maybe this is the way it was always meant to happen. Christian scholar Beatrice Bruteau believes this: "I think that we must see our technology as something holy . . . the vital advancing edge of the symbiotic cosmos."[6] Could it possibly be that the universe is unfolding exactly as it should?

Evolutionist Barbara Marx Hubbard thinks so. She believes strongly in the power of choice, and has spent most of her life dedicated to the human potential, teaching the importance of each of us taking responsibility for our beliefs. She explains her vision this way:

> "The effort to develop a new meme is a vital aspect of feeding the hungry, healing the sick, stopping the violence and freeing the world of poisonous toxins. The most direct path to our survival and fulfillment is to develop and communicate an idea system that guides us toward ethical evolution. In the past, memes arose unconsciously and

directed our actions, often without our knowing it. But now we are responsible not just for our actions, but for our beliefs as well. Common sense dictates that we evaluate our beliefs on the basis of how they affect us. If they make us more loving, creative, and wise, they are good beliefs. If they make us cruel, jealous, depressed, and sick they cannot be good beliefs and we must remove them from our consciousness. We need to take responsibility for what we believe."[7]

And this is exactly what we do. We weave the web with visionary beliefs, building a model of reality for ourselves that reflects all that is good and noble. We sculpt ourselves with consciousness for the betterment of our species. If one out of a thousand of us chooses this vision and acts in these ways, we can change the world.

Conscious evolution is presently birthing evolutionary artists from every culture, artists who are telling their stories in a variety of ways. It is often the artists, mystics and visionaries who feel it first, who create the inspiring visions that call us to action. When these ideas find themselves in mass-media productions such as big-budget movies—which they have—we know it is already in the collective unconscious, and is soon to be conscious for us all. This is what is so exciting and thrilling about our times. Inspirational theatre, music, books and films are lifting the vision of humanity, helping us to see ourselves in a new way in this the greatest and most exciting time to be alive, the time of the Great Awakening, where our species evolved to cosmic consciousness.

Slowly the memes of conscious evolution and each of us counting for a thousand will propagate and gather momentum until millions of us feel the authenticity of this vision, and we find ourselves thinking and acting in ways that surprise us. Evolutionary forces are at work, calling out to us, and many of us are feeling this call and acting, each in our own unique way, and this is why there is such hope for the future.

The changes will be small, almost imperceptible at first, but as the tide gains strength many more will feel it too and be inspired to act. Our species has been programmed for just this opportunity, and many surprises are in store for us once we hit critical mass. When seven million of us act in quantum ways, we will weave the web with images that will be unstoppable.

This is where quantum warriors are called to action. We have a vision of what is possible and are prepared to live for it. Physicists may have the knowledge and understanding of the mechanics of the universe, but the warrior takes this knowledge and lives it. It is the active 'living of these truths' that distinguishes warriorship from other practices. This is an important point. It is also the difference between the paths of the mystic and the warrior. A mystic may perceive the universe in a non-Newtonian way and feel his oneness with it, but he rarely acts in a proactive way to create changes. He is content to influence the collective with the vibration of who he is, which indeed is a necessary and valuable contribution. The quantum warrior however, not only vibrates the web with who she is but further contributes by focusing her will and imagination in ways that her highest calling reveals. Quantum warriorship is a new discipline for today's world. It is the vision, complete with a methodology, of becoming an integrated human being assisting humanity into cosmic consciousness. It is our calling to awaken, fulfill our potential and be our best.

WHAT IS POSSIBLE

We need to think revolutionary thoughts, thoughts so visionary and inspiring that they break through the restraints of our incredulity and shock us with their daring and vision. This is the only way to transform ourselves and the world. Nobel laureate Muhammad Yunus painted one such scenario to a group of us in Vancouver, a vision that seemed unimaginable. You might be aware that Yunus won the Nobel Prize for inaugurating the first microloan program for the poor, where loans of several hundred dollars or less are given to the poorest of the poor to help establish them in small business ventures. When you're desperate and have nothing, living day by day, getting a loan to buy a donkey or a sewing machine can be a huge hand up. The program is a resounding success that yearly helps hundreds of thousands of people through affiliate programs around the world. This is an extraordinary accomplishment, but the vision that so inflamed me was when Yunus said, "One day in the future, when there is finally no more poverty on the earth, they will build museums to show future generations what poverty was like, and these future generations will be horrified that people could allow such things to happen."[8]

It wasn't the eradication of poverty that was so incredible to me, as I can imagine this happening, but that they would have museums to show poverty to future generations, that these generations would be horrified that those of us in the past (you and me) allowed this to happen; that really shook me. Something inside me shifted and I saw it. I saw museums in the future displaying conditions of poverty, and future generations reacting with horror, and I knew in that instant that this vision was possible. And if it is possible, then I have a social responsibility to assist it happening by choosing to believe in this vision and weaving it into the web. Each of us has a social responsibility to choose visions that empower our species. There must be a critical number of us thinking this way if we are to advance.

When cosmic consciousness births itself it will change not just our own lives, but the very fabric of humanity, every part of life as we now know it. Evolutionary religion will be swept along with the rising tide. Spiritual leaders of all faiths will join together and find common ground to serve the spiritual needs of their people. Whatever your present spiritual belief or metaphysical preference, this will surely evolve into something grander, deeper, something fresh and alive, something never before experienced on this planet. The great religions and faiths that have served mankind for thousands of years will not be discarded in this new evolutionary change, but rather they will be reinvigorated from within, as our changing consciousness sweeps away rigid dogma and the spirit of what is at the core of all religions—the oneness of us all—blossoms forth.

So too with medicine, business, politics; they will all be transformed. What staggering changes will sweep through these activities? All we can say with certainty is that they won't look anything like they do today. Imagine the sweeping changes that will come when conscious evolution takes hold, and we feel our oneness as something so obvious that to separate ourselves into haves and have-nots would be as ludicrous as cutting off our hands and feet. Imagine when we are led, nurtured and inspired by the most visionary and brightest in all fields of human activity. The brightest and smartest are now mostly preoccupied with wealth and power, and who can blame them; these are fine and worthy prizes in the monopoly game. But imagine when these individuals and others of equal or greater capabilities discover the cosmic game as well, and feel a deep calling to make this world a better place, not because they think they should but because it becomes the most obvious thing to do. Suddenly they realize there is nothing they would rather do, and they do it with vision and passion. Imagine the smartest and brightest, millions of them, using their vision, wealth and talent in creative ways to help the disadvantaged, the poor, the elderly, the young and promising. Imagine them taking on causes, creating opportunities and succeeding in everything they do. And they will succeed, for these are the brightest and smartest our race has produced. Imagine them working in visionary ways, dedicated to the betterment of mankind. Imagine a world like this. Can this happen? It will happen. Evolution will make it happen.

When the memes of conscious evolution and each of us counting for a thousand take hold, many will be moved to action. This vision could help a drug addict stop shooting heroin, or whatever substance has captured him, because he believes his act counts for a thousand others and he sees how this act could make a difference, not just to him but to many. It gives him inspiration and courage, and in freeing himself he becomes a warrior. The corrupt businessman, inspired by this vision or perhaps haunted by a dream which reveals his dark shadow, or maybe a sacred wound that cracks him open (for these too are evolution in action), changes his ways. Suddenly he feels called, inspired, and he begins integrating himself into his community, building homeless shelters, giving grants to the disadvantaged, discovering himself in a whole new way. A single mother, desperate, fearful, with no hope, is inspired by this vision, uplifts herself, and this act of courage too weaves the web, helping others. The vision spreads and many people act in meaningful ways, each of them counting for a thousand. These memes become a vision of hope and inspiration, and many embrace them, until the critical number is finally reached and the shift occurs.

It is possible that cosmic consciousness will happen this way, or in another way that none of us yet knows. We are in uncharted waters here, but make no mistake: the tides have shifted from ebb to flow and the currents are running swiftly. This is not the time to procrastinate. We are being given an opportunity to participate in something extraordinary. Cosmic consciousness is knocking at our door, and some of us must have the courage to open the door and venture out into what is calling us.

All great revolutions of the past have happened because a few individuals, fired with a vision of what is possible, decide to act. It always begins with a few, but the few become many when the conditions are ripe. What is different this time, however, is that this is no ordinary revolution, a changing of the guard so to speak; this is the caterpillar becoming the butterfly. This is the extraordinary evolution of our species into cosmic consciousness. This is a calling worthy of our full attention, and we need seven million of us playing the cosmic game for something profound to happen.

Lung-ya, the great Zen Master wrote a beautiful poem:

> Those in the past who were not
> enlightened will now be enlightened;
> You ought to acquire this in this very life.
> When Buddhas were not enlightened, they
> were like you are now;
> If you become enlightened now, you will
> be like the old Buddhas.[9]

This poem inspires us. It tells us that not only is Buddhahood possible, but that all the old Buddhas were once just like us—procrastinators, putting off making commitments, concerned with our material comforts, worried over trivial matters, doubting ourselves. It is encouraging to know that they too struggled before enlightenment, that in fact they were just "like you are now." And then they became Buddhas!

Jesus encourages us to do this as well. In what I think is the most explosive and radical scripture in the Bible, Jesus tells us to be just like him. I have quoted this scripture in the previous chapter. In John 14:12, Jesus tells us that whatsoever things he does we can do also "and greater works" will we do.[10]

It is this passage more than any other that leads me to believe that Jesus understood the coming conscious evolution. My Christian friends are sometimes uncomfortable when I speak this way, but it is written in the Bible and we can't just ignore it, pretending it isn't there.

We have to assume that Jesus knew exactly what he was saying, and if this is the case extraordinary things are about to occur on this planet.

When you get over how outrageous this all is, it suddenly makes so much sense. The universe has been evolving and changing ever since the big bang, and now we are in a hyperenergetic time where something extraordinary is about to happen. The universe is unfolding in a grand cosmic design that is beyond our present ability to comprehend, and each of us, along for the ride, is playing our own unique role in this evolution. Cosmic consciousness is presently birthing itself in our species, and the most outrageous part about it is that if we play our cards right, master the cosmic game and awaken ourselves, we might even get to play in all of eternity. Now that could be fun.

THE JOURNEY CONTINUES...

A 20-PART PODCAST
SERIES BY JOHN KEHOE

"THE PATH OF THE QUANTUM WARRIOR"

WWW.QUANTUMWARRIOR.ORG

NOTES

Chapter One: Mind Power

1. From Einstein to Stephen Hawking the view of the universe is continually expanding. These aspects of the universe are just a few of the numerous startling revelations available to 21st century science. While there is presently much speculation about the nature of dark matter and dark energy, there is so little known or understood about these particular aspects of our universe that I have chosen not to address them. There are many references used in the compilation of this book, however, the main physicists I have relied on as a foundation for the scientific part of this work are Stephen Hawking, Brian Greene and David Bohm.

2. The *Elegant Universe*, PBS miniseries 2003.

3. It is only in the last quarter-century where actual scientific proof verified the effects of consciousness on energy. One of the hundreds of experiments that helped establish this was facilitated by Robert G. Jahn at Princeton University, with the results verified by the prestigious U.S. National Research Council in 2000. I reference this experiment in the text.

4. Depth psychology focuses on the relationship between the conscious and unconscious mind. The term refers to the continuing development of theories and psychoanalytic therapies based on the work of Pierre Janet, William James, Sigmund Freud and Carl G. Jung. There are so many talented individuals working creatively with consciousness that depth psychology could now be considered one of the most exciting and innovative fields of scientific discovery.

5. All parts of our universe are connected and part of one whole. This is the premise postulated by physicist David Bohm and now widely accepted. Physicists refer to this phenomenon as interconnectivity.

6. This is one of the most extraordinary aspects of quantum reality. Two books that simplify the enigmatic nature of time are *Introducing Time* by Craig Callender and Ralph Edney (Icon books, 2004) and *The Yoga of Time Travel* by physicist Alan Wolf (Quest Books, 2004). While there are more scholarly publications available, these will assist the average reader to understand time as nonlinear.

7. One of the early experiments that established the relationship between intention and physical reality was conducted by Robert G. Jahn at Princeton University in 1979.

8. The book *Mind Power*, rereleased in 1997 as *Mind Power into the 21st Century*, was first released in New Zealand while I was on tour. I remember checking the

bestseller list, which came out every Sunday, and discovering to my amazement it was number one. I called almost everyone I knew blurting out, "I know New Zealand is a tiny little island in the middle of nowhere but I'm number one here." This was followed by a release in Australia where it spent three months on the bestseller lists, and it went on to become a bestseller in numerous countries, including the United States, eventually selling over two million copies worldwide.

9. Quantum reality is the reality that exists beyond our five senses. It is the world of the infinitely small where subatomic particles transcend into energy and all things exist in an energy field. Quantum theory, which describes quantum reality, was first postulated by Niels Bohr and further elaborated upon by many physicists including David Bohm, whom I reference in this book. Physicists presently use a combination of Einstein's relativity theory, quantum theory and string theory to describe our reality.

10. Kabbalistic teaching (see chap. 2, n. 4).

11. Quantum models are the interpretations we use to make sense of the reality we are experiencing. In truth they are choices, for there are many ways of interpreting our reality.

12. The quantum vacuum is what scientists term the "first cause" in that everything comes from this source. It is the energy source behind all things. As will be discussed in this book, we feel a more accurate description would be to call it the "second cause," with consciousness being the first cause.

13. The specific vibrational energy that defines and identifies everything in the universe. Each 'thing' in the universe has its own particular energy signature, which 'informs' and distinguishes it from everything else.

14. When I began working with these principles in the mid 1970s there was very little scientific proof that we could in fact interact with energy in the ways I was attempting. We are fortunate today to have the scientific proof verifying our ability to direct energy with consciousness. This gives us the confidence to use these methods knowing they are having an effect.

15. The subconscious will accept whatever patterns are presented to it through repetition. The French psychologist Émile Coué (1857–1926) was one of the first investigators to discover the power of using the will and the imagination together to influence the subconscious. He achieved extraordinary results in assisting patients to heal themselves using these methods. Because we are a microcosm of the macrocosm we can access and direct any energy in the universe through intention and imagination.

16. I have described my first time speaking in public in the book *The Practice of Happiness*. It was a disaster. I forgot everything I was going to say and was overcome with stage fright. Fortunately I worked through these first few pitiful

attempts and eventually became a very skilled orator. In my early attempts I used to pray that I would be as good as my material, which I knew was excellent. Now I'm as comfortable being in front of a thousand people as I am talking one on one. My prayer became a reality.

17. TV personality and movie actor Jackie Gleason once said, "Everyone should have two fortunes in their life. One to blow and one to keep." I had never had large amounts of money before, so during the early years I spent it lavishly, freely, even recklessly. Fortunately, this period of being "crazy with money" lasted for only five or six years, but it was fun at the time and I have great memories. Let me also add, there was also a lot of "spillage" in that friends, artists and charities also benefited extremely well during this era. Abundance was flowing and many benefited.

18. It started out as a two-year sabbatical, but it was increased by an extra year because of a dream I had towards the end of the second year.

Chapter Two: Consciousness

1. Norman Doidge, *The Brain That Changes Itself* (New York: Penguin Group, 2007), 196-200.

2. Doidge 201-203.

3. Invented in 1947 by physicist Dennis Gabor, a hologram is made by using a laser to record and later reproduce what appears as a three-dimensional image, much like sound recordings that are digitally encoded in order to be reconstructed later.

4. An ancient Jewish mystical tradition, Kabbalah is characterized by beliefs about the nature of divinity, the origin of the soul, and the role of human beings. The word Kabbalah is derived from a Hebrew term that means "what is received" or "from tradition."

5. Parables were designed to illustrate or teach some truth, religious principle or moral lesson. They were a common method of teaching in ancient times. As complex truths could be reduced to simple stories, within each parable there were layers of meaning and insights which required further contemplation and understanding in order for them to be fully grasped. This is something mostly forgotten in today's approach to these teachings. Often they are accepted as either literal truths or dismissed as simplistic. Both these approaches fail to give the reader the depth of understanding the parables are meant to convey.

6. Doidge 294.

7. The well-known phrase "Neurons that fire together wire together" is paraphrased from: "When an axon of cell A is near enough to excite cell B and repeatedly

or persistently takes part in firing it, some growth process or metabolic change takes place in one or both cells such that A's efficiency, as one of the cells firing B, is increased." From D. O. Hebb, *The Organization of Behavior: A Neuropsychological Theory* (New York: John Wiley & Sons,1949). One of the first people who suspected the brain had neuroplastic capabilities was Sigmund Freud, who described a phenomenon called transference when he observed that memories thought forgotten could reappear as actions. Basically the brains of his patients had "moulded" themselves to these memories or experiences. Sigmund Freud first proposed the concepts behind Hebb's law, "Neurons that fire together wire together."

8. Doidge 222-225.

9. Daniel Siegel, *The Developing Mind: How Relationships and the Brain Interact to Shape Who We Are* (New York: Guilford Press, 1999), 20.

10. Ibid.

11. The system refers to the dynamics of both the conscious and subconscious minds collecting information and forming models of reality.

12. The collective unconscious is the part of the mind that is rarely perceived at the level of awareness occurring beyond the level of the conscious mind yet still has an influence on behavior.

13. My wife had a traumatic experience as a young girl of five where she was left in a toy store and watched from the window as her parents, brothers and sisters drove away without her. This sense of abandonment could have been assimilated in many ways. My wife, shortly after this incident made a conscious decision to be "so talented and great" that her parents would never leave again. This resulted in her being an extraordinary achiever in everything she does. She is a remarkably talented woman, and this one incident became a major influence in who she has become.

14. John Bruer, *The Myth of the First Three Years: A New Understanding of Early Brain Development and Lifelong Learning* (New Jersey: Simon and Schuster, 1999).

15. Some of these scientists include, Helen Neville of the University of Oregon, Phillip Shaver of the University of California and Richard Davidson of the University of Wisconsin.

16. Sharon Begley, *Train Your Mind Change Your Brain* (New York: Ballantine Books, Random House, 2007), 112-113.

17. Doidge.

Chapter Three: Quantum Reality

1.   Quantum theory is a branch of physics providing a mathematical description of the wave-particle duality of behavior in the interaction of matter and energy. Quantum mechanics describes the time evolution of physical systems via a mathematical structure called the wave function. The wave function has several solutions that give the probability of the system's state found at a given time.

2.   String theory is a theory in particle physics that attempts to reconcile quantum mechanics and general relativity. This theory attempts to describe fundamental forces and matter in a mathematically complete system.

3.   M-theory is an extension of string theory in which eleven dimensions are identified and the weak and strong forces of gravity are unified. This theory unites all five string theories and describes low-entropy dynamics also known as supergravity interacting with two- and five-dimensional membranes.

4.   Some famous proponents of string theory include Edward Witten, Juan Maldacena, Leonard Susskind, Brian Greene and Stephen Hawking.

5.   Niels Bohr, Werner Heisenberg, Max Planck, and others established the foundations of quantum mechanics in the early 20th century. In 1925, Bohr and Heisenberg published results that closed the old quantum theory. From Einstein's postulations, there was a flurry of debate, theorizing and testing leading to modern quantum mechanics, which included the concept of a wave-particle duality.

6.   Lynn McTaggart, *The Field: The Quest for the Secret Force of the Universe* (UK: HarperCollins Publishers, 2001), 11.

7.   The double-slit experiment first postulated by Thomas Young in 1803, and reproduced many times with more and more sophistication, proves the strange nature of molecular particles. Basically, a subatomic particle is fired at a screen with two slits cut within it. The patterns that are produced beyond the slits indicate that the particle must be both a wave and a particle at the same time. However, whenever quanta are observed through sophisticated instruments they always appear to be particles. It is now well established in the scientific community that the act of observing somehow influences what quanta become.

8.   McTaggart 111-117. Also Michael Talbot, *The Holographic Universe* (New York: HarperCollins 1991), 122-126.

9.   Dean Radin, *Entangled Minds* (New York: Simon & Schuster, 2006), 154.

10.   George Wald, "Life and Mind in the Universe," *International Journal of Quantum Chemistry* 26, no. 11 (1984): 1-15.

11.   Theoretical physicist and cosmologist Alan Guth is the originator of the inflationary universe theory.

12. *The Elegant Universe*. Dir. Joseph McMaster and Julia Cort. Perf. Michael Duff, Michael Green, Brian Greene, Walter Lewin, and Joseph Lykken. NOVA, 2004. Documentary.

13. Peter N. Spotts, *Christian Science Monitor* 93, no. 218 (2001): 15.

14. "Holographic Memory: Karl Pribram," Interviewed by Daniel Goleman, *Psychology Today* 12, no. 9 (1979): 72.

15. Holomovement is a key concept in Bohm's interpretation of quantum mechanics, which brings together the holistic principle of the universe as an undivided whole. This includes the idea that everything is in a state of becoming or universal flux.

16. Michael Talbot, *The Holographic Universe* (New York: HarperCollins, 1991), 52.

17. Talbot 51.

18. Gareth Knight, *A Practical Guide to Qabalistic Symbolism* (Samuel Weiser Publishers, 1978), 175.

19. Matt. 6:33, The Holy Bible: King James Version (Iowa Falls, IA: World Bible Publishers, 2001). The terms "kingdom of heaven" and "kingdom of God" seem to be interchangeable, with Matthew using mostly kingdom of heaven and Mark, Luke and John using kingdom of God.

20. The Gospel of Thomas, 113.

21. Francis Dojun Cook, *How to Raise an Ox* (Los Angeles: Center Publications, 1979), 82.

22. It could be argued that Max Planck as early as 1900 was the father of what was to be called quantum theory. There are dozens of scientists who have contributed to this theory.

23. Used in Zen Buddhism, a koan is a riddle or dialogue of question without a logical answer. The meaning of a koan cannot be understood by rational thinking but is accessible only through meditation and intuition. Through prolonged meditation over a period of months and even years one receives a flash of insight which reveals the answer to the koan. Rōshi Philip Kapleau describes koans this way: "The great merit of koans . . . is that they compel us, in ingenious and often dramatic fashion, to learn these doctrines not simply with our head but with our whole being, refusing to permit us to sit back and endlessly theorize about them in the abstract."

24. Combining quantum mind power with neuroplasticity gives us ways of re-creating ourselves never before practiced. As we change ourselves in this way, we literally become "new beings."

25. http://quoteworld.org.

Chapter Four: The Mythology of a Quantum Warrior

1.   James Hillman, *Re-Visioning Psychology* (New York: Harper Paperbacks, 1977), 154.

2.   Chogyam Trungpa, *Shambhala: Sacred Path of the Warrior* (Bantam Books, 1984), 8.

3.   Ezra Pound, *The Spirit of Romance* (New York: New Directions, 2005), 93.

4.   Cook 9.

5.   Heinrich Zimmer, *Philosophies of India,* ed. Joseph Campbell (Princeton, New Jersey: Princeton University Press, 1969), 542.

6.   David Feinstein and Stanley Krippner, *The Mythic Path: Discovering the Guiding Stories of Your Past – Creating a Vision for Your Future* (New York: G. P. Putnam's Sons, 1997).

Chapter Five: Beliefs

1.   A prosperity consciousness is a consciousness that has an abundance vibration. It is created by thinking prosperity thoughts. Our subconscious holds many belief patterns within it. A prosperity consciousness is fuelled by the thoughts and beliefs of abundance, success and prosperity which we entertain on a conscious and subconscious level.

2.   From Matt. 21:22.

3.   Since the publication of "The Powerful Placebo" (1955), the phenomenon has been considered to have clinically significant effects.

4.   Henry Beecher, "The Powerful Placebo," *Journal of the American Medical Association* 159, no. 17 (1955): 1602-1606.

5.   *New England Journal of Medicine* 347 (2002): 81-88.

Chapter Six: Athletes of the Mind

1.   Jim Murphy, personal conversations, 2009.

2.   Aryeh Kaplan, *Meditation and Kabbalah* (Boston: Red Wheel/Weiser, 1982), 113.

3.   Ibid. 112.

4.   A Freudian technique of allowing words and thoughts to come out spontaneously without filtering them for meaning or direction.

5.   Kaplan 113.

Chapter Seven: Weaving the Web

1. Jack Canfield, *The Success Principles* (New York: Harper *Collins, 2005*), 57, 75.

2. Carl G. Jung, *Synchronicity: An Acausal Connecting Principle* (Princeton: Princeton University Press, 1969).

3. I believe this was Ira Progoff who spent extensive time with Jung, however, at the time of publication I was unable to source the exact reference.

4. Mystery Wisdom Workshop presented by Jean Houston in Washington, DC, 2003.

5. http://writerspages.net.

6. Joseph Campbell and Bill Moyers, *The Power of Myth* (New York: Doubleday, 1988).

7. Johann W. V. Goethe, *Maxims and Reflections of Goethe* (New York: The MacMillan Company, 1906).

Chapter Eight: The Subconscious

1. Sylvia Bak is a filmmaker and mystic. She is also my wife. Most mornings we sit in our bedroom overlooking the ocean and mountains, in conversation for at least an hour before we begin our day. It was during one of these conversations when she came up with the quote at the beginning of this chapter. I immediately wrote it down because I thought it was one of the best descriptions of the subconscious that I had heard. Actually, on mornings when she is inspired and on a roll I become what she calls "the scribe," dutifully recording furiously.

2. Doidge 179-188.

3. Robert Bly, *A Little Book on the Human Shadow* (New York: HarperOne, 1988).

4. Matt. 25:14-30.

5. Carl G. Jung, "Psychology and Religion," *Collected Works of C. G. Jung, Volume 11 Psychology and Religion: West and East* (New Jersey: Princeton University Press, 1938), 131.

6. In Castaneda's books Don Juan does not actually use the words collective unconscious, conscious and subconscious but refers to the *tonal,* the world of material objects, and the *nagual*, the nonmaterial world, however, it is clear what he is referring to. An excellent book that interprets Castaneda's methodology with the Jungian system is *Border Crossings: A Psychological Perspective on Carlos Castaneda's Path of Knowledge* by Jungian analyst Donald Lee Williams.

Chapter Nine: Listening

1. Ahmadou Kourouma, *Waiting for the Wild Beasts to Vote* (Vintage U.K. Random House, 2004).

2. Mark Hedsel, *The Zelator: A Modern Initiate Explores the Ancient Mysteries* (Random House, U.K. 1998).

3. Antonio Damasio, *Descartes' Error* (London: Quill, 1995), 212-226.

4. Ibid.

5. Walt Whitman, "Song of Myself," *Leaves of Grass* (New York: Bantam Dell, 2004).

6. Ceremony is simply an elaborate way of working with energy. The subconscious responds to dramatics, and the more elaborate the imprinting method the better. While religions and shamanistic traditions have used ceremony for thousands of years, the ability of working with this method is available to anyone who understands the dynamics of consciousness and energy.

7. Psychodrama is a psychological technique whereby inner aspects of the psyche act themselves out in roles.

8. "The Snow Man," *The Great Modern Poets,* ed. by Michael Schmidt (UK: Quercus Books, 2010), 43.

9. "Quantum Healing, Consciousness and Soul" series hosted by Shifra Hendrie, July 2010.

10. Harmon H. Bro, *Edgar Cayce on Dreams* (New York: Warner Books 1968).

Chapter Ten: The Seven Disciplines

1. Philip Kapleau, *The Three Pillars of Zen* (London: Rider & Co. Ltd., 1965), 183.

2. Brother Lawrence of the Resurrection (c. 1614–12 February 1691) served as a lay brother in a Carmelite monastery in Paris. His teachings are collected in *The Practice of the Presence of God* by Father Joseph de Beaufort.

3. There are many methods of meditation. Active meditation is the act of engaging in deep thought or reflective contemplation. The practitioner trains their mind into a mode of consciousness in order to realize some benefit. This is the way of the quantum warrior. Passive meditation is stilling the mind from its incessant thinking of thoughts. Both are extremely valuable in training the mind.

Chapter Eleven: Quantum Time

1.   The 'twin paradox' is a thought experiment in special relativity that has received much attention in the physics community. For example, Einstein, Born and Møller invoke gravitational time-dilation to explain the movement of time based upon the effects of acceleration.

2.   Philip K. Dick, "How to Build a Universe That Doesn't Fall Apart Two Days Later." 1978. <http://deoxy.org/pkd_how2build.htm>.

3.   I have found in my spiritual work that the universe is very generous in giving us what we want when we show the initiative and make our intention clear.

4.   Talbot 226-228.

5.   Robin Banks is a leading authority on mind power and is a highly sought-after international speaker. Robin mentored with me in the late '90s and began teaching my course in 2003. He is an extraordinarily gifted individual and plays monopoly with the skill of a warrior.

6.   Michael Brooks, "Entanglement: The Weirdest Link." *New Scientist*, 181(2004): 32.

7.   Napoleon Hill, *Think and Grow Rich* (New York: Ballantine Books, 1960), 215-218.

8.   Andrew Harvey and Mark Matouske, *Dialogues with a Modern Mystic* (New York: Quest Books, 1994).

9.   Jean Houston's Mystery School Workshop, Oregon 2002.

10. Vedas are a large body of texts originating in ancient India composed in Vedic Sanskrit. This text contains the oldest scriptures of Hinduism.

11. Bhagavad Gita is a Hindu scripture considered among the most important texts in the history of literature and philosophy.

12. From Matt. 26:34.

13. Stephen Hawking, *A Stubbornly Persistent Illusion: The Essential Scientific Works of Albert Einstein* (Philadelphia: Running Press, 2007).

Chapter Twelve: Creating a Model of Reality

1.   *Maya* in Hinduism deals with the concept of "illusion", and *Maya* is the principle deity that manifests or perpetuates the illusion and dream of duality in the phenomenal universe.

2.   John 14:12. The scripture states: "Verily, verily, I say unto you, He that believeth on me the works I do shall he do also; and greater works than these shall he do;

because I go unto my Father." I have substituted "ye" for "he" for the flow of the narrative. Believing in Jesus is living his teachings, which I have pointed out in this text are in complete agreement with possibilities presented by quantum theory. There are some who might argue only those who become religious and follow the Christian teaching will experience this, but I feel Jesus is being more inclusive and is encouraging all of us to use his life as a template and to claim our natural God-given talents. We are asked to believe in what he is teaching and his life serves as a demonstration of what is possible for all of us. It is this belief, which gives us the opportunity to take it further. The main point of this scripture, which makes it so explosive, is he is telling us that "greater things" will we do if we follow this method. Greater things! Christians and non-Christians alike must digest this proclamation and decide to either accept or reject this teaching. If we decide to accept it, the implications of what we are called to do and become are staggering.

3.   John 10:30.

4.   Matt. 5:48.

5.   Some scholars speculate that Hermes Trismegistus is the combination of the Greek god Hermes and the Egyptian god Thoth, both being gods of writing and magic.

6.   Clement Salaman, Dorine van Oyen, William D. Wharton, Jean-Pierre Mahé, *The Way of Hermes* (Rochester: Inner Traditions, 2000), 57-58.

7.   Isaac Luria (1534-1572) was a prominent rabbi and Jewish mystic who is considered to be the father of contemporary Kabbalah. He gave a revolutionary new account of Kabbalistic thought.

8.   The Zohar is the foundational work in the literature of Kabbalah containing a discussion on the nature of God and our souls, as well as the origin and structure of the universe.

9.   Kaplan 203.

10. Jeffrey M. Schwartz and Sharon Begley, *The Mind and the Brain: Neuroplasticity and the Power of Mental Force* (New York: HarperCollins, 2002).

11. Gerhard Dorn, *The Speculative Philosophy*, trans. by Paul Ferguson (Glasgow: Adam McLean publisher, 1979).

12. Dion Fortune, *The Mystical Qabalah* (Maine: Samuel Weiser, 1993), 188.

13. *The Essential Rumi*, New Expanded Edition, trans. by Coleman Barks (New York: HarperCollins, 1995).

14. The original drawings and the commentary that accompanies them are both attributed to Kuo-an Shin-yan (Kakuan Shien), a Chinese Zen master of the 12th century.

15. Kapleau 323.

16. Ibid.

17. Matt. 23:11.

18. Matt. 25:35-45.

19. Matt. 22:39.

20. Matt. 14:44-46.

21. Cook 45.

22. Knight.

23. Cook 6.

24. Matthew Fox, *The Coming of the Cosmic Christ* (San Francisco: HarperCollins, 1983).

25. Kapleau 323.

26. Sun Bear was a teacher and visionary, a medicine chief of the Bear Tribe.

Chapter Thirteen: Conscious Evolution

1. Perhaps the most well known theologian to articulate this premise would be Matthew Fox, in his book *The Coming of the Cosmic Christ.*

2. 2 Pet. 3:10.

3. Edgar Mitchell, *The Way of the Explorer* (Career Press 2008) and Institute of Noetic Sciences, <http://www.noetic.org>.

4. Agnes De Mille, *Martha: The Life and Work of Martha Graham* (New York: Random House, 1991).

5. Howard Bloom, *The Lucifer Principle* (New York: Atlantic Monthly Press, 1997). Concept 3 from 5 main concepts.

6. Barbara Marx Hubbard, *Conscious Evolution: Awakening the Power of Our Social Potential* (Novato: New World Library, 1998), 59-60.

7. Hubbard, 83-84. Plus private conversations.

8. Muhammad Yunus Lecture (Vancouver: Chan Center, March 14, 2008).

9. Cook 113.

10. See chap. 12, n 2.

SELECTED BIBLIOGRAPHY

Begley, Sharon. *Train Your Mind Change Your Brain*. New York: Ballantine Books/Random House, 2007.

Bohm, David. *On Creativity*. New York: Routledge, 1996.

———. *Thought As a System*. New York: Routledge, 1992.

Callender, Craig and Ralph Edney. *Introducing Time*. UK: Icon Books, 2004.

Campbell, Joseph and Bill Moyers. *The Power of Myth*. New York: Doubleday, 1988.

Cook, Francis Dojun. *How to Raise an Ox*. Los Angeles: Center Publications, 1979.

Doidge, Norman. *The Brain That Changes Itself*. New York: Penguin Group, 2007.

Feinstein, David and Stanley Krippner. *The Mythic Path: Discovering the Guiding Stories of Your Past–Creating a Vision for Your Future*. New York: G. P. Putnam's Sons, 1997.

Fortune, Dion. *The Mystical Qabalah*. Maine: Samuel Weiser Inc., 1993.

Fox, Matthew. *The Coming of the Cosmic Christ*. San Francisco: HarperCollins, 1983.

Greene, Brian. *The Elegant Universe*. New York: Vintage Books/Random House, 1999.

Hawking, Stephen and Leonard Mlodinow. *The Grand Design*. London: Bantam Press, 2010.

Hubbard, Barbara Marx. *Conscious Evolution: Awakening Our Social Potential*. California: New World Library, 1998.

Kaplan, Aryeh. *Meditation and Kabbalah*. Boston: Red Wheel/Weiser, 1982.

Kapleau, Philip. *The Three Pillars of Zen*. London: Rider & Co. Ltd., 1965.

Knight, Gareth. *A Practical Guide to Qabalistic Symbolism*. Maine: Samuel Weiser Publishers, 1978.

Laszlo, Ervin and Jude Currivan. *CosMos: A Co-creator's Guide to the Whole-World*. New York: Hay House Inc., 2008.

Laszlo, Ervin. *Science and the Akashic Field.* Vermont: Inner Traditions, 2004.

Leonard, George. *Mastery: The Keys to Success and Long-Term Fulfillment.* New York: Penguin Group, 1992.

Lipton, Bruce. *The Biology of Belief: Unleashing the Power of Consciousness, Matter and Miracles.* California: Elite Books, 2005.

Loori, John Daido. *Riding the Ox Home.* Boston: Shambhala Publications Inc., 1999.

McTaggart, Lynne. *The Field: The Quest for the Secret Force of the Universe.* UK: HarperCollins, 2001.

————. *The Intention Experiment.* New York: Free Press/Simon & Schuster, 2007.

Pagels, Elaine. *The Gnostic Gospels.* New York: Random House, 1979.

Pearce, Joseph Chilton. *Magical Child.* New York: Bantam Books, 1977.

Progoff, Ira. *Jung, Synchronicity, and Human Destiny.* New York: Dell Publishing, 1973.

Radin, Dean. *Entangled Minds: Extrasensory Experiences in a Quantum Reality.* New York: Simon & Schuster, 2006.

Salaman, Clement, Dorine van Oyen, William D. Wharton, and Jean-Pierre Mahé, trans. *The Way of Hermes: New Translations of the Corpus Hermeticum and the Definitions of Hermes Trismegistus to Asclepius.* London: Gerald Duckworth & Co., 1999.

Schwartz, Jeffrey M. and Sharon Begley. *The Mind and the Brain: Neuroplasticity and the Power of Mental Force.* New York: HarperCollins, 2002.

Sheldrake, Rupert. *Morphic Resonance.* Vermont: Inner Traditions, 1981.

Stapp, Henry P. *Mind, Matter and Quantum Mechanics.* New York: Springer-Verlag Berlin Heidelberg, 2004.

Talbot, Michael. *The Holographic Universe.* New York: HarperCollins, 1991.

Williams, Donald Lee. *Border Crossings.* Toronto: Inner City Books, 1981.

Wolinski, Stephen. *Quantum Consciousness: The Guide to Experiencing Quantum Psychology.* Connecticut: Bramble Books, 1993.

www.learnmindpower.com

John Kehoe invites you to visit his website and continue with your exploration of the human potential. It contains articles, important news, podcasts, videos, interesting links, and is an invaluable source of relevant information. Updates on what John is working on as well as his most recent articles and tour schedule are regularly posted.

Other books by John Kehoe

Mind Power into the 21st Century
Mind Power for Children
A Vision of Power and Glory
Money, Success & You
The Practice of Happiness

SEMINARS AND WORKSHOPS
WITH JOHN KEHOE

John Kehoe conducts workshops and seminars worldwide.

John Kehoe's Mind Power Training
The once a week, 4-week Mind Power Training is now being taught by John's protégé Robin Banks, and is also available as a home study program. The 10-CD program, recorded live in 2001, is the complete 4-week Mind Power Training system that John taught around the world for twenty-five years. Students can now train at home with John as their personal teacher, learning the essential techniques to manifest the life they desire.

Quantum Warrior Training
An introductory seminar into the path of the Quantum Warrior.

The Awakening
A five-day "live-in" workshop where participants integrate mind, body, subconscious and soul to awaken to their full potential. Completion of the Mind Power Training is a prerequisite.

The Initiation
A five-day "live-in" workshop where the advanced techniques of quantum warriorship are developed and experienced. Completion of the Mind Power Training and the Awakening are prerequisites.

For more information about these workshops and to register: www.learnmindpower.com/seminars